Literature Puzzles for Elementary and Middle Schools

LITERATURE PUZZLES
for
Elementary and Middle Schools

CAROL J. VEITCH
and
CECILIA M. BOKLAGE

Illustrated by
Patricia A. Mannerberg

LIBRARIES UNLIMITED, INC.
Littleton, Colorado

1983

LIBRARIES UNLIMITED, INC.
P.O. Box 263
Littleton, Colorado 80160-0263

Library of Congress Cataloging in Publication Data

Veitch, Carol J., 1942-
    Literature puzzles for elementary and middle schools.

    Bibliography: p. 103
    Includes indexes.
    1. Literary recreations. 2. Crossword puzzles.
3. Word games. 4. Educational games. I. Boklage,
Cecilia M., 1946-   . II. Title.
GV1493.V44 1983   793.73   82-20847
ISBN 0-87287-363-3

REPRODUCTION RIGHTS

For all our loved ones,
with thanks for their support and patience

PREFACE

Literature Puzzles for Elementary and Middle Schools has been designed to supplement the upper elementary, middle, or junior high school literature program by providing enrichment activities in the form of seek-a-word and crossword puzzles for 25 popular titles. Titles selected for this puzzle book come from a wide range of literary genres and readability levels. Newbery Award winners and runners-up are well represented in the puzzle selections. The authors have made a conscious effort to include titles which would be widely available in most library collections serving grades 4-8.

The words and illustrations for each of the seek-a-word puzzles have been chosen from the individual book's incidents or characters. For students who have read the book from which the puzzle was derived, the puzzle will assist the student in recalling these characters and events. For students who have not read a particular book, the puzzle can be used to arouse interest as the words suggest interesting events in the book.

The crossword puzzles have been developed to reinforce the student's memory of incidents and characters in each book as the clues directly relate to these. For this reason, the crossword puzzles probably will not be successful with students who have not read the book to which the puzzle relates.

Puzzles in *Literature Puzzles for Elementary and Middle Schools* can be used equally well by classroom teachers, school librarians, and children's or young adult public librarians for individual students or groups of students. Some of the ways the puzzles might be used include:

1. Whole class activity after the teacher or librarian has read the book to the class or after the class has studied the book in the literature program. The crossword puzzle might substitute for a test on the book in the latter case.

2. As an activity center in the library or classroom for individual students to work as they choose. Puzzle pages could either be duplicated or laminated. Displaying the book(s) in the center will serve as a further enticement to read or reread the book(s).

3. A transparency of the puzzle page with answers marked would enable a student to check his/her answers quickly. Posting a laminated answer sheet near the activity center would also allow the student to check answers easily and independently.

4. Public and school librarians could duplicate puzzle pages to distribute to library users in conjunction with summer reading programs or to promote other special reading activities or events.

5. The crossword puzzles might serve as a substitute for traditional book reports as the student would have to read the book before he/she could do the puzzle.

6. Puzzles, especially the seek-a-word puzzles, could be used as a special treat before holidays or other times when a break in the routine is desirable.

7. Younger students can also color in the illustrations after they have worked a seek-a-word puzzle.

8. Puzzles are effective and enjoyable devices for teaching problem-solving techniques, thus reinforcing other curricular objectives. The seek-a-word puzzles are especially effective for developing search strategies, helping students see letter patterns within words, and challenging students to find words hidden in the puzzles. Crossword puzzles are especially effective for developing recall of specific events and characters in the books, increasing vocabulary, and using word recognition skills to help fill in puzzle blanks.

9. The puzzles could serve as a springboard to student-designed puzzles for other books which they have enjoyed reading and would like to share in this way with classmates. Puzzles in *Literature Puzzles for Elementary and Middle Schools* could be utilized as examples of literature-based puzzles. The design of puzzles is creative and teaches students to think about books in terms of important characters and events, etc., as students must choose the words and clues for their own puzzles. Puzzle-making might easily substitute for traditional book reports as students would have to read the book carefully before a puzzle could be developed effectively. (Puzzle creation can also teach students much about patience, persistence, and the need for frequent revision if the original ideas don't work!)

This book includes both a crossword puzzle and a seek-a-word puzzle for each title. Answers to the puzzles appear in a separate section at the back of the book.

The suggested grade-level index is intended only as a guide for titles which might not be familiar to persons using this puzzle book. The grade-level index is in no way intended to limit the use of any puzzle. Many of the titles can be used with gifted students/voracious readers in grades lower than those suggested, while slower students/reluctant readers in upper grades might find some of the easier titles appealing. As with all materials, the teacher or librarian must be guided by his/her knowledge of the particular book and the interests of the individual student or class. For the purposes of this puzzle book, the grade-level designations were developed from the author's experience as a middle school librarian and from consultation with other librarians and classroom teachers. Puzzle difficulty was, in some degree, geared to these grade-level suggestions.

All of the suggestions for using *Literature Puzzles for Elementary and Middle Schools* are designed to get you started thinking about ways YOU can use the books and puzzles with your students. They are only starting points. Happy puzzling!

Carol J. Veitch

ACKNOWLEDGMENTS

No book just happens. Many people besides the authors and illustrator play important roles in the creation of a book. We would like to take this opportunity to publicly thank some of these special people.

Jane Crawford for preparing the answer pages to the seek-a-words.

Charles Boklage for his assistance with the crossword puzzle graphics.

Patricia Higson for typing and proofreading various parts of the manuscript.

Rebecca Hurdle and Sharon Smith, graduate teaching fellows at East Carolina University, for proofreading and other assistance.

Heather Cameron and Ann Hartman, Libraries Unlimited editors, for their patience and support.

Teachers and librarians who tested puzzles in their classrooms and libraries.

Everyone else who in any way contributed to this book.

Carol J. Veitch
Cecilia M. Boklage
Patricia A. Mannerberg

TABLE OF CONTENTS

PUZZLES

PUZZLES

The Black Stallion
By Walter Farley

SEEK-A-WORD

```
S T O R M S R O S I A T K W Y
E Y R E T S Y M E H L K R E O
A R Y C A P E P T W L R O N O
R S E N E H A E L L E S Y A G
C A R I G C D E L D C H W I C
H R C C S N I A I N I A E R T
A E S E H K T R A I N I N G C
P E W H I S T L E E S L C G A
A C S H R I N N M L T U H N E
E E L I E L E O A Y A C I I S
C L K O S R G N R B L A C K O
A C C N C S D N Y H L D A N R
A S E N U T E E R E I I G D M
L T A L E H A R Y R O S O S R
B P O N A P O L E O N L A T E
```

WORDS:

Alec	New York
Black	Race
Chicago	Rescue
Escape	Ride
Henry	Search
Herd	Stall
Island	Stallion
King	Storm
Mystery	Training
Napoleon	Whistle

The Black Stallion

By Walter Farley

CROSSWORD

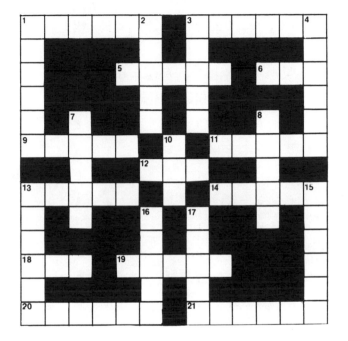

ACROSS

1. Cyclone and Sun _____ were the Black's rivals.
3. The Black did not like the feel of a _____ on his back.
5. The Drake sank in the Atlantic _____.
6. The part of a bridle that goes into the horse's mouth.
9. It had been twenty _____ since Henry rode in the Derby.
11. The Black jumped the _____ wall when frightened by a monoplane.
12. Black's _____ was injured in the Chicago race.
13. The wild horse pulled Alec to an island not more than two _____ in circumference.
14. Kentucky Derby winners receive a horseshoe of _____.
18. The Black's favorite game was _____.
19. The Drake's hold was filled with a _____ of rice, tea, and jute.
20. Alec caught fish at the island with handmade _____.
21. Alec used Henry's old _____ saddle.

DOWN

1. Alec's last name.
2. Alec found carragheen growing on the island's _____.
3. Henry put the Black in the _____ next to Napoleon.
4. Alec kept the Black in an old barn behind a run-down _____.
7. Joe Russo worked for the _____ TELEGRAM.
8. Chang was a race _____.
10. Alec's hair was _____.
13. Alec was away from home for five _____.
15. The shelter Alec built was near the only _____ on the island.
16. Alec had to finish his _____ before he could go to Chicago.
17. The Black liked to eat lumps of _____ from Alec's hand.

Blubber
By Judy Blume

SEEK-A-WORD

```
B  M  A  I  L  B  O  X  L  L  O  O  H  C  S
O  W  E  A  E  N  B  B  U  R  W  I  R  E  M
L  L  U  L  F  R  E  A  E  E  J  L  L  P  E
A  G  E  A  H  W  H  S  T  R  F  R  L  O  L
H  H  A  T  A  S  N  N  S  T  E  A  E  U  L
M  A  T  M  L  E  E  L  I  L  S  P  H  G  Y
T  E  S  O  L  C  I  L  N  B  O  X  O  P  K
P  S  S  F  O  C  L  L  I  J  A  M  O  R  O
T  E  G  S  W  H  I  N  H  I  S  T  E  S  T
L  R  A  G  E  L  S  S  C  G  E  B  R  I  L
B  F  I  L  E  O  C  P  A  G  B  E  A  A  E
Y  B  A  A  N  I  K  P  M  U  P  L  I  B  N
A  H  R  T  F  O  O  B  L  A  F  R  O  O  Y
W  P  I  L  L  O  W  B  I  H  T  O  R  E  S
N  K  P  O  K  E  R  D  S  R  E  S  W  I  P
```

WORDS:

Baby
Blubber
Closet
Diapers
Eggs
Fat
Flenser
Halloween
Jill
Laugh

Machinist
Mailbox
Poker
Pumpkin
Report
School
Smelly
Stamps
Trial
Whale

Blubber

By Judy Blume

CROSSWORD

DOWN

2. The school bell finally _____ as Linda finished her report on whales.
3. Tracy's costume was _____ Bird from Sesame Street.
4. Jill and Tracy decided while raking leaves that Mr. Machinist had funny _____.
5. The photographer wanted to _____ a picture of Jill and Linda while they lit the thirteenth candle.
7. Great Aunt Maudie made them eat wheat germ _____ for breakfast.
8. Wendy _____ to the principal about Blubber and the chocolate-covered ant.
10. Jill wore one of her mother's _____ for part of her flenser costume.
11. The school nurse told Linda to go on a _____.
13. The girls made Blubber _____ Wendy's sneaker.
14. Jill and Tracy didn't know Mr. Machinist had _____ them on Halloween.
17. Jill painted her _____ boots gold.
19. Mr. Vandenburg made a _____ of multiplication facts for Tracy's class.

ACROSS

1. The Brenners were late for Warren Winkler's _____ mitzvah.
4. Tracy and Jill cracked raw _____ in Mr. Machinist's Mailbox.
6. Linda had a _____ tooth.
7. Mr. Machinist sent the Halloween photo through the _____.
9. At the Country Club, Kenny ate Jill's _____ because she didn't like vegetables.
10. Caroline _____ Linda's hands behind her back to make her eat a chocolate-covered ant.
12. Blubber's _____ was shaped like a potato.
13. Caroline found the _____ to the supply closet in Mrs. Minish's desk.
15. Two sixth-grade boys made _____ balls and shot them at Linda on the bus.
16. Wendy wanted to get _____ with Jill for ending Blubber's trial.
18. Jill made a _____ saying "Flenser" in case people didn't recognize her Halloween costume.
20. Jill loved to _____ peanut butter.

The Bridge to Terabithia
By Katherine Paterson

SEEK-A-WORD

```
M  D  G  C  S  N  E  I  R  R  E  T  G  D  F
T  I  I  S  T  E  E  E  D  E  O  E  D  A  R
E  R  S  A  L  C  R  K  S  E  C  R  E  T  M
A  E  T  S  G  A  L  L  E  R  Y  A  R  F  T
J  R  O  E  E  A  E  G  D  I  R  B  I  S  E
P  I  R  V  S  D  P  G  A  S  D  I  I  N  M
I  B  I  O  T  I  M  L  H  E  R  T  Y  A  G
H  V  E  R  R  L  L  O  G  Y  R  H  G  O  R
S  E  S  G  O  J  E  L  N  A  A  I  U  N  D
D  L  I  L  S  S  C  S  P  D  C  A  R  E  R
N  E  S  E  E  A  R  S  L  E  S  C  U  R  A
E  M  A  M  S  S  E  D  N  I  S  T  G  O  D
I  G  R  T  S  E  E  O  T  S  E  R  S  T  A
R  A  L  I  I  G  K  N  O  R  I  E  U  E  E
F  E  C  M  M  P  L  A  Y  G  R  O  U  N  D
```

WORDS:

Artist	Jess
Bridge	Leslie
Castle	Magic
Creek	Miss Edmonds
Dead	Playground
Dog	Run
Farm	Secret
Friends	Stories
Gallery	Terabithia
Grove	Terrien

The Bridge to Terabithia

By Katherine Paterson

CROSSWORD

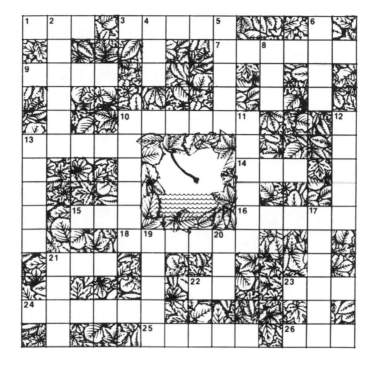

ACROSS

1. May Belle wanted _____ special doll for Christmas.
3. Jess made a funeral wreath in the pine _____.
7. _____ became Jess' friend.
9. Jess liked to _____, "mostly crazy animals with problems."
10. The season of the year when Leslie moved next door.
13. Leslie gave Jess a _____ set for Christmas.
14. Jess' sisters always wanted to buy _____ clothes.
15. Jess' age.
16. Leslie and Jess swung on a rope to _____ Terabithia.
18. Miss Edmunds played the _____.
21. Terabithia was a secret king_____.
22. Nickname Leslie gave her dog.
23. The seventh-graders considered the back of the _____ "their" territory.
24. _____ Avery was a bully.
25. The boys at Lark Creek School ran _____ each day at recess.
26. Her classmates thought Leslie was _____ because she had no TV.

DOWN

2. Jess and Leslie read the _____ books.
4. When Jess was embarrassed, he turned _____.
5. One of Jess' sisters.
6. _____ Bessie was a cow.
8. Mr. Aarons had only one _____.
10. Their castle _____hold was made of boards from the scrap heap.
11. Leslie was the fastest _____ in fifth grade.
12. Rain filled the creek bed with _____.
13. Jess gave Leslie a _____ for Christmas.
17. Miss _____s was the only teacher who wore jeans to school.
19. Jess hid his sketch pad and pencils _____ his mattress.
20. Miss Edmunds took Jess to an _____ gallery.
21. When Jess returned from Washington, he found out Leslie was _____.

Charlotte's Web

By E. B. White

SEEK-A-WORD

```
F  O  T  T  N  O  T  E  L  P  M  E  T  S  F
C  E  E  W  S  A  T  U  M  I  B  T  P  A  W
H  A  R  I  V  S  N  O  H  L  L  E  I  I  I
R  L  L  N  E  R  T  I  E  E  E  R  L  D  V
S  R  A  D  I  A  N  T  L  H  N  B  E  E  R
N  B  A  S  T  U  A  C  A  F  U  R  R  S  M
O  U  S  T  A  L  A  R  U  R  N  S  Y  E  I
I  R  W  P  D  R  A  Y  N  R  A  B  T  R  A
T  E  F  C  I  R  R  I  I  T  T  T  E  L  C
A  B  A  M  F  D  F  F  I  E  O  H  R  R  H
T  I  E  G  G  S  E  L  N  L  E  A  R  T  U
U  R  B  C  T  E  E  R  R  R  Y  U  I  E  M
L  A  A  G  W  E  B  A  I  P  N  S  F  S  B
A  S  R  I  A  R  H  G  V  T  G  G  I  I  L
S  N  Y  P  D  C  E  G  R  T  E  A  C  L  E
```

WORDS:

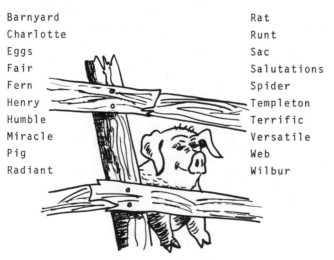

Barnyard   Rat
Charlotte   Runt
Eggs   Sac
Fair   Salutations
Fern   Spider
Henry   Templeton
Humble   Terrific
Miracle   Versatile
Pig   Web
Radiant   Wilbur

Charlotte's Web

By E. B. White

CROSSWORD

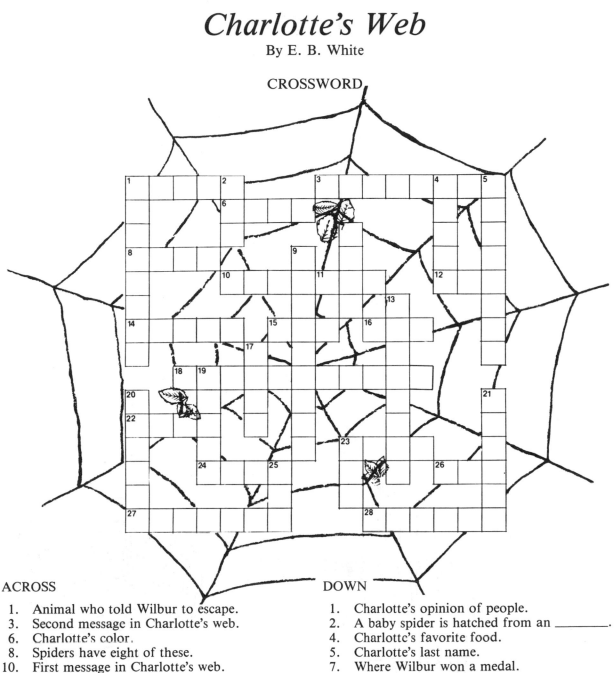

ACROSS

1. Animal who told Wilbur to escape.
3. Second message in Charlotte's web.
6. Charlotte's color.
8. Spiders have eight of these.
10. First message in Charlotte's web.
11. Wilbur was a _____.
12. Goose _____ on her eggs and hatched seven goslings.
14. The Zucherman's hired hand.
15. One of Charlotte's children.
16. The pouch Charlotte spun.
18. Charlotte's greeting to Wilbur.
22. Wilbur's home was the manure _____.
23. The girl who adopted Wilbur.
24. Charlotte lived less than one _____.
26. Charlotte's _____.
27. Third message in Charlotte's web.
28. Fern's last name.

DOWN

1. Charlotte's opinion of people.
2. A baby spider is hatched from an _____.
4. Charlotte's favorite food.
5. Charlotte's last name.
7. Where Wilbur won a medal.
9. Charlotte's babies made balloons and sailed away on updrafts because they were _____.
13. The animals lived here.
17. Mr. Arable's description of Wilbur at birth.
19. Name of Fern's brother.
20. Charlotte was a _____.
21. Fourth message in Charlotte's web.
23. Templeton was very _____ after his night at the fairgrounds.
25. Templeton was a _____.

Dorp Dead

By Julia Cunningham

SEEK-A-WORD

```
W   W   I   N   D   O   W   D   G   E   A   O   L   O   T
I   D   G   G   A   D   Y   L   L   I   D   P   K   R   O
N   O   O   T   N   M   R   G   I   C   L   H   N   P   B
D   W   E   E   C   A   E   P   O   R   L   L   A   H   A
G   O   R   R   A   O   T   D   K   C   R   O   Y   A   L
I   L   Y   N   G   T   N   O   W   E   O   E   C   N   O
P   L   A   R   E   H   U   D   H   C   R   R   I   K   S
H   L   N   U   E   L   H   T   A   E   L   C   R   P   P
M   A   S   H   R   T   O   N   N   R   E   W   O   T   E
L   D   D   T   O   M   I   O   G   E   U   N   L   S   U
A   D   E   A   D   W   S   W   H   M   T   A   P   C   E
E   E   D   N   E   I   E   O   O   C   B   A   R   O   L
R   R   A   L   R   R   K   L   U   O   S   I   O   A   K
K   R   O   P   M   A   A   N   K   P   N   P   D   E   N
G   B   A   H   S   H   N   I   A   T   N   U   O   M   A
```

WORDS:

Ankle
Cage
Clock
Dead
Dog
Dorp
Gilly
Grandmother
Hunter
Kobalt

Ladder
Mash
Mountain
Orphan
Peace
Prisoner
School
Soup
Tower
Window

Dorp Dead

By Julia Cunningham

CROSSWORD

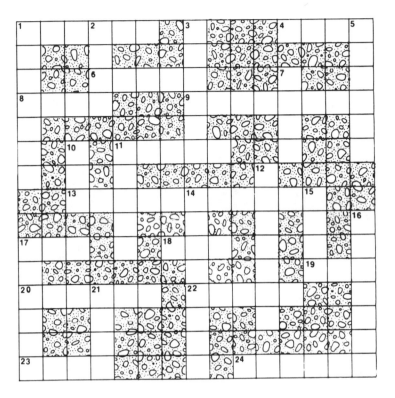

ACROSS

1. The _____ adopted Gilly.
4. The word Gilly always misspelled.
6. Gilly injured his _____ when he fell.
8. Gilly made _____ for dinner.
9. Small towns.
11. Gilly's job was to _____ the wood planks.
13. Before she died, Gilly lived with his _____.
17. The hunter's _____ was always empty.
18. Gilly used a wool _____ to extinguish the fire (for his escape).
19. Mash's color.
20. Gilly was an _____.
22. Gilly's refuge was a ruined _____.
23. Where Gilly wrote his last message to Kobalt.
24. There were fifteen _____ in Kobalt's house.

DOWN

1. Mrs. _____ ran the orphanage.
2. The tower became a _____ when Kobalt followed Gilly.
3. Gilly's age.
5. The stone house became Gilly's _____.
7. What Gilly saw when he looked in Kobalt's window.
10. Mash was a _____.
11. What Gilly was searching for.
12. Gilly escaped through the _____.
14. Location of Gilly's refuge.
15. Kobalt's _____ was always locked.
16. Kobalt made these.
17. Gilly's last name.
21. The one good _____ in Gilly's day was his free period.

The Egypt Game

By Zilpha Snyder

SEEK-A-WORD

```
E E E L C A R O S S E F O R P
E C E R E M O N Y O C L E S Y
Y A A E C U I D L C C E C E R
E L L I M N R E T A I R R A
L I A F C M A G E O H N E O M
A F O S Y Y A S M P R S M M I
S O R H S S I Y U Y A I M D
H R N E S O D L A S P T T E S
E N S E R E G I R X P P I U S
S I M A N O E O D Y T O T U T
M A A P R I L N G A C L R M C
G E G E F E M E L A N I E E O
R P I E R E R E D R U M F L M
O H R M A R S H A L L I E R P
F T S S I T I E S N E C N I A
```

WORDS:

April
California
Ceremony
Egypt
Eyelashes
Game
Hieroglyphics
Incense
Marshall
Melanie

Message
Mummy
Murderer
Nefertiti
Octopus
Oracle
Professor
Pyramids
Set
Yard

The Egypt Game

By Zilpha Snyder

CROSSWORD

ACROSS

1. The Egypt gang decorated the altar of Nefertiti with flowers, beads, and pretty _____.
4. The hieroglyph for Horemheb was a _____.
8. Marshall _____ the Professor watching the gang from his store window.
10. April's father died in the Korean _____.
11. Mrs. Ross served April a hot _____ sandwich for her first lunch with Melanie.
13. _____ was the Evil One, the god of Black Magic.
14. A period of history; The Egypt Game was based on the _____ of the Pharoahs.
15. Melanie, April, and Marshall _____ away from the group of trick-or-treaters.
17. The altar of _____ was a broken bird bath.
18. Set's altar was made from an _____ crate.
19. Melanie was afraid that the Wilson kids wouldn't stand for April's Hollywood _____.
22. Marshall was excited because he rode home in a police _____.
24. Marshall was Mr. Ross' _____.
27. When April first met Melanie, she was wearing Dorothea's old _____ stole.
28. April and Elizabeth were _____ girls at school that year.
29. The Professor's lean-to shed became an Egyptian _____.
30. April's code name was _____, the cat goddess.

DOWN

1. The Professor told a _____ story to the Egypt gang.
2. The Egypt gang had _____ altars in their temple.
3. At the drugstore, April bought false lashes for her _____.
5. Melanie's code name.
6. A female sheep.
7. A rodent related to the mouse.
9. Elizabeth became the Queen _____.
12. The sixth-grade teacher at Wilson.
13. According to April and Melanie, the _____ were the worst enemies of Egypt.
14. The children went trick-or-treating on All Hallows' _____ (Halloween).
16. Ken said he felt like a _____ playing the Egypt Game.
20. They found a metal mixing _____ to use as a firepit for sacred fires.
21. _____ Rosada.
22. Caroline _____ April's hair in a Cleopatra bob.
23. A form of the verb "be."
25. The two murders were committed by _____ person.
26. Used for landing fish.

27

Freaky Friday

By Mary Rodgers

SEEK-A-WORD

```
F  R  E  A  K  Y  F  R  H  A  P  C  E  M     N
R  C  I  S  W  O  L  L  A  M  H  S  R  A  M
I  O  B  R  S  O  G  E  L  R  I  O  R  O  E
D  N  D  R  Y  K  A  E  E  R  O  E  T  S  S
A  F  A  Y  A  F  B  F  O  M  A  H  H  S  S
Y  E  A  N  N  C  E  B  H  Y  E  N  M  E  Y
B  R  L  A  P  O  E  C  M  R  S  O  A  H  L
E  E  L  M  M  T  T  S  E  D  I  K  W  T  L
E  N  A  E  S  I  L  S  Y  N  R  H  S  O  O
C  C  R  C  W  E  O  A  F  U  O  O  B  L  E
A  E  O  S  B  C  A  O  C  A  F  C  E  C  Y
F  M  O  A  N  E  F  L  A  L  F  K  E  K  L
E  O  N  N  D  I  E  D  I  N  N  E  R  C  O
P  N  F  E  N  N  E  T  M  F  K  Y  N  O  H
A  R  E  E  R  B  P  C  O  C  O  F  F  E  E
```

WORDS:

Annabel	Freaky
Ape Face	Friday
Beet Loaf	Laundry
Boris	Legos
Braces	Marshmallows
Camp	Messy
Clothes	Mother
Coffee	Nok Hockey
Conference	Room
Dinner	Switch

Freaky Friday

By Mary Rodgers

CROSSWORD

ACROSS

1. Mr. Dill thought Annabel had lots of "spunk and _____."
3. Annabel's mother.
5. Ellen's middle name.
7. Max was the Andrews' _____.
9. Annabel thought that "McGuirk" rhymed with "work, shirk, and _____."
11. Mrs. Andrews smoked _____ packs of cigarettes a day.
13. The washing machine made so much _____ from the jacks and sneakers.
16. Annabel's hair was _____, just like her mother's.
18. Annabel's mother had Annabel's hair _____, which was an improvement.
19. Annabel thought Max's _____ tasted better than the meals at school.
21. Mrs. Schmauss drank the gin that was left on the _____.
22. Annabel was very _____ for her conference.
23. Boris returned the _____ his mother had borrowed.
24. Ben was _____ years old.

DOWN

2. Everyone except Annabel thought her room looked like a _____ pen.
3. Annabel had fun putting on lots of _____ make-up the morning she became her mother.
4. "Missing Persons" told Annabel to dial her _____ precinct.
5. One of Annabel's friends.
6. Boris thought he was playing _____ Hockey with Mrs. Andrews.
7. Boris cooked beet loaf for _____.
8. _____ was the cop who was not talking on the telephone.
10. Annabel was afraid that she had _____ her mother, her brother, and herself.
12. Another of Annabel's friends.
14. Mr. Andrews wanted Mrs. Andrews to _____ his shirts.
15. Annabel did not understand the "2:30" entry in her mother's _____ book.
17. Annabel let Ben put _____ jelly on his meatballs.
18. Mrs. Schmauss found an apple _____ under Annabel's bed.
19. Annabel received a bad report in _____ her classes except gym.
20. Ben's nickname was "_____ Face."
21. Annabel forgot to meet Ben's _____.

From the Mixed-Up Files of Mrs. Basil E. Frankweiler

By E. L. Konigsburg

SEEK-A-WORD

```
F  R  U  N  A  W  A  Y  A  I  D  U  A  L  C
N  R  E  I  M  A  J  T  A  I  R  F  A  C  A
I  E  M  L  H  E  N  L  P  T  E  T  E  N  F
A  M  L  I  I  F  E  G  O  O  T  I  M  I  E
T  M  P  X  C  E  X  D  E  I  N  K  E  L  T
N  U  E  M  T  H  W  A  Y  L  I  L  G  O  E
U  S  H  O  Y  H  A  K  I  E  R  E  U  I  R
O  E  T  O  O  S  S  E  N  T  I  R  A  V  I
F  U  M  U  C  C  T  T  L  A  Q  N  R  U  A
I  M  E  D  I  H  H  E  W  A  R  M  D  V  M
L  Y  O  U  R  E  R  E  R  O  N  F  A  W  A
E  L  F  E  I  A  E  S  F  Y  X  G  W  C  R
S  E  C  R  E  T  T  S  T  A  T  U  E  D  Q
F  A  K  N  F  R  A  W  E  I  L  L  S  L  O
M  I  X  E  D  U  P  A  N  Z  Y  G  E  L  O
```

WORDS:

Angel
Cafeteria
Cheat
Claudia
Files
Fountain
Frankweiler
Guard
Hide
Jamie

Michaelangelo
Mixed-up
Museum
Mystery
Run Away
Secret
Statue
Toilet
Violin
War

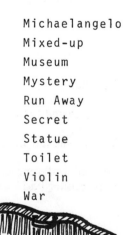

From the Mixed-Up Files of Mrs. Basil E. Frankweiler

By E. L. Konigsburg

CROSSWORD

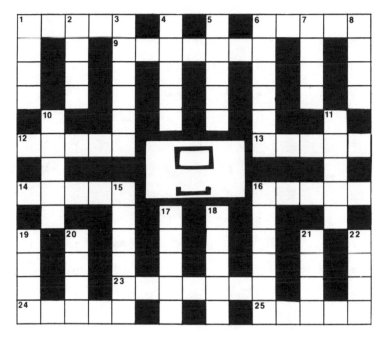

ACROSS

1. Claudia and Jamie found three stonemason's _____ on the velvet.
6. "_____ drift like clouds in an undecided breeze."
9. Jamie hid his _____ case inside an urn.
12. Claudia had _____ brothers.
13. Jamie and Claudia _____ up each evening and hid in separate washrooms.
14. "War" is played with _____.
16. Claudia chose Jamie to go with her because he had lots of _____.
23. Claudia rented a box at Grand _____ Post Office.
24. Claudia and Jamie ate _____ in the museum snack bar.
25. The mummies were in the _____ Room.

DOWN

1. There are two _____ of the museum in the book.
2. Mrs. Frankweiler was very _____.
3. Angel was a _____.
4. An embalmed body that has been preserved for thousands of years.
5. Claudia and Jamie _____ all their money on the taxi ride to Mrs. Frankweiler's.
6. Michelangelo was one of _____'__ most famous sculptors.
7. Jamie chose the _____ numbers on Claudia's list of file categories.
8. Claudia wanted to wear an Indian _____ like the U.N. guide.
10. The way Jamie won his card games.
11. Claudia found the sketch of Angel in Mrs. Frankweiler's _____.
15. Mrs. Frankweiler willed the _____ to Claudia.
16. Angel was carved from _____.
17. Claudia was very good at making _____ for them to follow.
18. A _____ stood at each of the museum's entrances.
19. Claudia was the only _____ in her family.
20. The state where the Kincaids lived. (abbr.)
21. New York _____.
22. Each child stood on a toilet _____ to hide.

Henry Reed's Journey

By Keith Robertson

SEEK-A-WORD

```
S  W  I  M  M  I  N  G  Y  E  N  R  U  O  J
E  S  W  M  R  G  E  N  Y  W  E  S  E  O  O
T  E  G  R  A  N  D  C  A  N  Y  O  N  N  U
I  I  G  O  M  A  A  G  D  O  O  W  D  E  R
M  N  U  O  L  L  I  G  M  L  Y  T  E  W  N
E  G  H  I  C  D  N  E  R  X  E  E  N  M  A
S  R  E  K  C  A  R  C  E  R  I  F  V  S  L
O  G  N  E  H  H  O  C  C  P  R  E  E  N  O
Y  N  R  N  I  G  F  O  H  H  T  T  R  A  C
O  I  Y  R  N  I  I  P  H  E  E  R  G  I  I
S  T  R  E  A  A  L  G  U  G  M  G  T  D  X
E  N  E  E  T  T  A  L  G  E  I  I  D  N  E
M  I  E  Y  O  O  C  U  G  L  B  B  S  I  M
I  A  D  D  W  C  N  W  E  L  E  L  T  T  M
T  P  A  I  N  E  W  M  E  X  I  C  O  C  I
```

WORDS:

California	Journal
Chemist	Journey
Chinatown	Midge
Denver	New Mexico
Firecrackers	Nugget
Giggle	Painting
Gold	Pueblo
Grand Canyon	Redwood
Henry Reed	Swimming
Indians	Yosemite

Henry Reed's Journey

By Keith Robertson

CROSSWORD

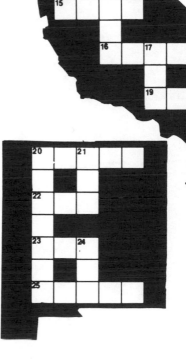

ACROSS

1. The _____ Canyon is in Arizona.
3. Los Angeles has many expressways for all the _____.
4. A cable _____ carried Henry and Midge to Fisherman's Wharf.
6. The abbreviation for mountain.
7. Midge wanted to set up a travel museum in her _____.
9. Amos was a _____ to Midge.
11. Henry had been away from the U.S.A. for one _____.
13. Abbreviation for South America.
14. Springfield is the capital of _____ (abbr.).
15. Midge and Henry were supposed to meet her parents at Disneyland's _____ gate.
16. Terry had four horned _____.
19. _____ Carson's house is in Taos, New Mexico.
20. Sequoias are giant _____.
22. The fat man _____ the shrimp sauce seasoned with Henry's hot pepper seeds.
23. _____ Vegas is in Nevada.
25. Cowboys ride broncos and steers in a _____.
26. Henry's plane landed in the state of _____ (abbr.).
29. The adventure with Diego the monkey happened in _____ Angeles.
31. Amy was a _____.
33. The men attending the convention in the Brown Palace Hotel wore _____ stetson hats.

DOWN

1. San Francisco's _____ Avenue is the heart of Chinatown.
2. Midge's Hopi name was _____ Rose.
5. The name of the poodle who liked women's shoes was _____.
7. Cindy, the girl from Chicago, screamed every time she saw a _____.
8. Henry wanted to be a _____ when he grew up.
10. Henry became a hero by suggesting _____ as a solution for lowering the swimming pool.
12. Henry had traveled all over Europe and part of _____.
17. Uncle Al said that strange things happened to Henry and his mother because they were "Great _____ people."
18. The fat man _____ on Henry in the cable car.
20. Mr. Glass bought a _____ to carry the freezer home.
21. Midge got a black _____ at Disneyland.
24. Terry was _____ when Midge and Henry left.
27. Henry was going to visit his Uncle _____ in New Jersey.
28. Big Trees _____ was in Yosemite National Park.
30. A homonym for "sew."
32. Midge started a _____ rush.
33. Midge filled a burlap _____ with pine cones.

Island of the Blue Dolphins

By Scott O'Dell

SEEK-A-WORD

```
O  I  S  A  B  A  L  O  N  E  E  S  A  I  S
L  T  O  R  H  B  B  T  T  E  A  P  L  E  L  H
A  N  T  A  O  M  A  R  R  A  O  E  F  D  A
B  F  D  E  E  L  O  T  R  N  O  A  E  I  B
E  L  T  P  R  U  H  C  E  E  A  V  V  U  A
C  O  U  S  D  Q  U  A  L  I  I  W  S  L  S
E  H  N  E  U  A  G  I  N  L  N  D  E  U  N
O  L  I  A  E  N  O  R  F  W  S  U  A  O  I
P  H  K  E  C  D  O  I  F  E  T  E  W  N  H
I  E  N  L  F  F  S  O  R  N  U  E  E  E  P
S  I  S  A  I  H  R  N  O  L  E  C  E  O  L
L  U  E  L  P  I  P  R  O  A  L  A  D  R  O
A  T  A  I  R  A  S  N  O  P  A  E  W  A  D
N  C  H  K  A  R  A  N  A  O  S  G  O  D  P
D  S  K  A  S  H  I  A  M  N  O  N  E  S  E
```

WORDS:

Abalone
Aleut
Alone
Blue
California
Canoe
Chief
Devilfish
Dogs
Dolphins

Earthquake
Island
Karana
Otter
Ramo
Rontu
Seaweed
Ship
Spear
Weapons

San Nicolas
(Island of the Blue Dolphins)

Island of the Blue Dolphins

By Scott O'Dell

CROSSWORD

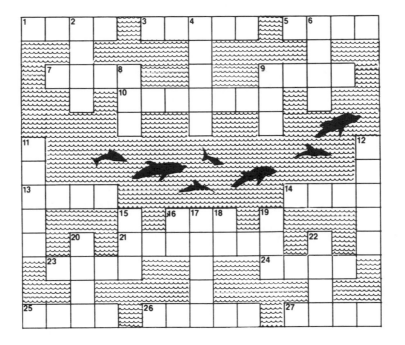

ACROSS

1. The sai-sai are small silver _____.
3. The white man _____ a dress for Karana from blue trousers.
5. The leader of the wild dogs had _____ hair and yellow eyes.
7. The cormorants roosted on _____ Rock.
9. _____ sinew was woven to bind things together.
10. The shellfish that were gathered at low tide and dried for winter food.
13. Karana's brother.
14. The Aleut ship sailed into Coral _____.
16. Karana named Rontu's son Rontu-_____.
21. The "devilfish" with many arms was probably an _____.
23. Karana tried to cross the sea to the country toward the _____.
24. The Channel Islands are in the Pacific Ocean between North America and _____.
25. The island did not have a single large _____, only small ones stunted by the wind.
26. Chief Chowig demanded _____ parts from the otter hunt.
27. The color of the dolphins.

DOWN

2. Karana _____ from the ship to the island to get Ramo.
4. Karana made her fence from _____ ribs.
6. Karana had two names, a "_____" one and one that was "common."
8. Tribal _____ forbade women to make weapons.
9. The Aleut's ship always crossed the _____ from the north.
11. Karana worked many days making a bow and _____.
12. The _____ ship had red sails.
15. Karana made a cooking _____ from a smooth stone with a hollow center.
16. Karana lived in the village of Ghalas-_____.
17. Karana's dog.
18. Karana climbed _____ the cliff face to escape from the tidal wave.
19. San Nicolas is a part of the _____ (country).
20. Karana kept the young birds in a reed _____.
22. The Aleut _____ gave Karana a black stone necklace.

Julie of the Wolves
By Jean George

SEEK-A-WORD

```
J  O  M  A  R  R  Y  Y  M  E  S  M  Y  A  I
Q  U  R  A  A  K  S  A  L  A  X  A  S  Y  A
E  S  L  M  M  N  R  R  O  M  K  A  E  C  E
I  L  O  W  A  E  J  U  W  Y  V  E  A  I  S
V  E  S  T  R  Q  T  L  E  H  F  R  L  M  I
E  A  U  W  O  L  V  E  S  T  I  U  U  T  R
K  R  I  Q  Q  U  N  I  E  B  J  O  A  A  E
E  M  F  O  M  H  W  E  O  W  H  T  S  N  U
E  U  A  Y  I  B  I  U  O  P  E  N  P  A  L
R  E  T  N  U  H  R  A  C  M  M  E  L  L  E
U  K  X  A  S  L  L  E  S  K  I  M  O  Q  M
T  A  W  K  Y  E  O  A  A  T  U  L  L  M  M
S  Y  E  L  A  M  I  Y  A  X  E  R  L  A  I
E  A  T  A  M  J  A  F  E  G  U  K  E  E  N
G  U  S  S  A  K  U  R  G  S  S  A  J  S  G
```

WORDS:

Alaska	Julie
Amaroq	Kayak
Amy	Lemming
Caribou	Marry
Eskimo	Miyax
Fur	Nature
Gesture	Penpal
Gussak	Seal
Hunter	Stew
Jello	Wolves

Julie of the Wolves

By Jean George

CROSSWORD

ACROSS

1. The name of a wolf pup.
3. Julie's father.
6. Eskimos depend on the _____ for food and clothing.
8. A sled is pulled by a _____ of dogs.
9. A small, simple hut; Julie built a _____ of sod.
12. The gray male wolf in Amaroq's pack.
13. A grasslike plant that helped Julie on her trek.
14. Frozen water.
15. Julie caught a snowy _____.
16. Daniel's mother.
18. Julie's memories of each scene in seal camp were a different hue or _____.
19. Rein_____ and caribou herds roam the Arctic tundra.
20. Julie named her plover, Tor_____.
25. A short sleep.
26. The people that live in the Arctic regions of North America.
27. One of the basic supplies Julie took with her in her backpack.

DOWN

1. Another wolf pup.
2. Julie made a _____ from frozen grass sticks and caribou skin.
3. The boats that Eskimos use.
4. The half-moon shaped knife used by Eskimo women.
5. Both days and _____ are light through the Arctic summer.
6. Used for transportation over the snow.
7. Julie's penpal.
10. _____ and Eskimos were taught at the Bureau of Indian Affairs School.
11. Eskimos dig _____ in the permafrost to store food.
17. A small, thin tool Julie used for sewing.
18. An "i noGotied" is one of many Eskimo magic objects or _____.
19. Snow during Arctic winters is very _____.
21. Julie used a homemade snare to _____ small animals for food.
22. Foxes and wolves live in a _____.
23. An Eskimo word of greeting or an exclamation of surprise.
24. Used to catch or trap fish.

Little House in the Big Woods

By Laura Ingalls Wilder

SEEK-A-WORD

```
Q  H  M  S  D  O  O  W  G  I  B  P  G  A
W  A  C  H  U  R  N  Q  L  G  A  O  R  R
I  R  T  A  O  O  W  G  I  N  X  L  A  U
S  E  I  R  O  T  S  R  T  N  W  G  G  A
C  L  B  V  U  X  B  H  D  D  U  G  D  L
O  X  A  E  G  N  E  L  E  S  H  R  O  O
N  T  E  S  D  R  D  I  E  X  G  C  L  T
S  A  R  T  Y  C  R  L  D  Q  I  L  L  X
I  B  E  A  R  R  P  Q  E  L  D  D  I  F
N  O  T  N  A  A  R  Y  A  B  W  F  M  Z
X  C  N  C  M  A  X  C  L  T  E  I  T  T
H  S  I  P  O  P  C  O  R  Y  L  D  R  X
Q  I  W  H  O  U  S  E  S  R  D  D  I  F
S  W  O  O  W  T  G  N  I  K  P  M  U  P
```

WORDS:

Bear	Maple Sugar
Big Woods	Mary
Calico	Pa
Carrie	Panther
Churn	Pumpkin
Fiddle	Rag Doll
Harvest	Stories
House	Trundle Bed
Laura	Winter
Ma	Wisconsin

Little House in the Big Woods

By Laura Ingalls Wilder

CROSSWORD

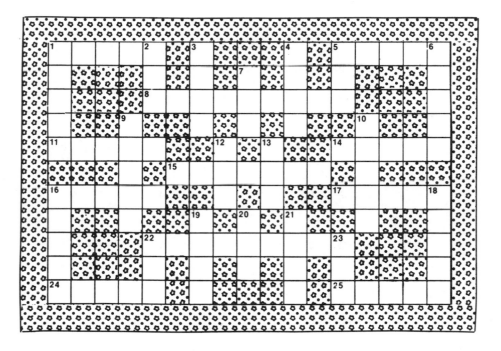

ACROSS

1. Laura and Mary made Christmas candy from molasses and sugar _____.
5. Charlotte and Nettie were rag _____.
8. The little house was in this state.
11. Sukey and _____ were cows.
14. Pa told Laura and Mary the _____ of Grandpa's sled and the pig.
15. Laura and Mary wore red _____ nightgowns in the winter.
16. The Ingalls lived _____ miles from town.
17. _____ Claus brought the children red mittens and peppermint candy.
22. Laura named her new doll _____.
24. In the winter, the best time of all was at _____ when Pa told stories and played his fiddle.
25. Pa greased his _____ by the fire in the evenings.

DOWN

1. Pa helped Grandpa collect sap after the _____ snow fell.
2. The bear drew out the honey from the bee tree with its _____.
3. Aunt Ruby wore a red _____ pin made from sealing wax.
4. Ma moved the churn-_____ up and down to make butter.
5. A bear's winter home is a _____.
6. Laura wrote her book about her own life _____ years earlier.
7. Laura lived in a _____ house.
9. Pa made soft leather from deer _____.
10. Ma made hats from _____.
12. Laura braided the straw to make a _____ for her doll.
13. Butchering Time marked the _____ of autumn and the beginning of the long winter.
16. Grandma stirred the boiling syrup with a wooden _____.
18. Ruby and Docia were Laura's _____.
19. Pa used _____ to cure the deer meat.
20. A type of tree found in the Big Woods.
21. Pa carved a big _____ on the top of Ma's wooden shelf.
22. Black Susan was a _____.
23. The children could _____ all the maple sugar they wanted at Grandpa's dance.

Mary Poppins
By P. L. Travers

SEEK-A-WORD

```
O  P  P  U  L  K  P  B  S  L  A  S  S  E  S
P  H  A  M  A  D  R  Y  A  D  P  S  I  T  W
H  Y  I  B  D  C  A  U  T  L  A  N  A  I  C
S  A  M  R  N  H  G  B  R  P  N  R  M  R  H
M  A  A  E  I  H  A  E  M  A  S  O  Y  D  A
B  A  R  L  W  L  L  O  N  H  C  R  O  C  L
D  E  N  L  T  E  C  A  I  A  E  B  L  I  K
M  R  R  A  S  E  M  H  C  S  A  M  E  H  P
Y  T  S  T  E  O  R  T  R  N  C  E  A  G  I
R  A  I  N  W  B  U  U  K  I  N  S  H  U  C
D  R  A  D  E  M  N  S  E  P  S  T  C  A  T
C  J  R  T  E  C  N  E  P  P  U  T  I  O  U
H  I  S  N  E  U  C  O  W  U  Z  A  M  O  R
B  A  N  N  I  A  R  E  S  T  R  O  Z  A  E
M  A  R  Y  P  O  P  P  I  N  S  S  O  L  S
```

WORDS:

Banks
Bert
Bird Woman
Chalk Pictures
Christmas
Compass
Cow
Hamadryad
Jane
Laugh

Mary Poppins
Michael
Nannie
Nursery
Stars
Tea
Tuppence
Umbrella
West Wind
Zoo

Mary Poppins

By P. L. Travers

CROSSWORD

ACROSS

4. The wind slipped under Mary Poppins' _____ and carried her away.
5. Mary Poppins slid _____ the banisters.
8. Admiral Boom's house was built like a _____.
9. John and Barbara Banks were _____.
11. Andrew was a _____.
14. The dancing cow jumped over this.
15. Katie _____ always smelled of barley water.
17. Mary Poppins' suitcase was a _____ bag.
20. _____ was very naughty one day.
22. The wind was blowing from the _____ when Mary Poppins left.
24. The hamadryad gave Mary Poppins his snake _____.
25. The children slept in the _____.
26. The oldest of the Banks children.

DOWN

1. Mary Poppins' _____ was on a full moon.
2. The Bird Woman sold bread crumbs for _____ a bag.
3. The wind was blowing from the _____ when Mary Poppins arrived.
6. Mr. Banks worked in the _____.
7. A _____ took the children around the world.
10. Each piece of gingerbread was topped by a gilt _____.
12. Green lights mean _____.
13. Mr. Wigg and the children were full of _____ gas.
16. The Banks family lived on _____ Tree Lane.
18. John put his _____ in his mouth to amuse the grown-ups.
19. Mrs. Corry had _____ daughters.
20. One of the Pleiades.
21. _____ painted chalk pictures.
23. A _____ party on the ceiling.

Misty of Chincoteague
By Marguerite Henry

SEEK-A-WORD

```
R  C  O  M  M  T  E  O  U  U  P  J  Y  P  B
D  C  H  I  N  C  O  T  E  A  G  U  E  E  L
N  A  S  M  G  D  A  Y  N  D  P  L  N  N  A
I  T  I  A  Y  L  U  E  S  O  N  Y  M  G  Z
Y  N  T  U  F  O  A  L  D  T  I  N  R  S  E
N  S  H  R  C  G  A  N  R  O  E  M  O  T  L
O  G  L  E  L  G  E  G  M  D  O  R  T  U  M
P  S  D  E  L  G  E  O  N  T  P  A  S  A  N
I  E  A  N  E  L  L  A  N  N  E  R  U  O  E
T  E  N  L  I  L  L  A  L  O  N  E  I  E  N
P  S  R  N  S  S  H  E  Z  A  O  L  G  E  F
H  N  R  P  I  P  O  A  M  A  L  E  C  D  L
A  O  R  O  U  N  D  U  P  A  N  A  L  B  U
N  O  E  L  L  A  G  Y  T  T  R  L  U  A  P
G  A  L  C  H  I  E  S  O  S  N  E  T  E  A
```

WORDS:

Blaze	Misty	Pony
Chincoteague	Oysters	Race
Foal	Paul	Round-up
Galleon	Penning	Stallion
Gold	Phantom	Storm
Island		
July		
Legend		
Mare		
Maureen		

Misty of Chincoteague

By Marguerite Henry

CROSSWORD

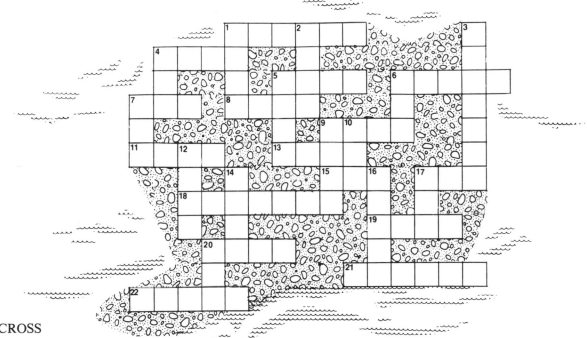

ACROSS

1. The wild ponies had _____ coats to keep them warm in winter.
4. Paul and Maureen made a _____ on the pully bone to see which one would ride Phantom in the race.
5. Maureen's brother.
6. The White _____ of Assateague were sand dunes.
7. The children earned _____ hundred dollars to buy the Phantom.
8. The _____ Piper was the lead stallion in his band of mares.
9. A young horse or pony.
11. Maureen saw a "sold" _____ around Misty's neck the morning after Penning Day.
13. The Fire Chief _____ Misty and Phantom to Mr. Foster.
15. Opposite of "subtract."
17. Grandpa agreed to give Maureen and Paul _____ dollars for each colt the children could halterbreak.
18. The _____ was the wild pony with a white map marking her withers.
19. Grandpa used a _____ when he walked.
20. The characters in *Misty of Chincoteague* were _____ people.
21. Chincoteague is an _____ off the coasts of Virginia and Maryland.
22. Grandpa's last name.

DOWN

1. A galleon is a type of _____ used most often during the sixteenth century.
2. Paul and Maureen were very _____ after they bought Misty.
3. The first ponies swam ashore after a Spanish _____ wrecked on the shoals.
4. The Phantom and Paul _____ the race.
5. The wild ponies were kept in _____ on Pony Penning Day.
6. Misty snatched a lady's _____ covered with roses and dropped it in a rain barrel.
7. Used to row a boat.
9. The ladies of the auxiliary served _____ fritters on Penning Day.
10. Strange or peculiar.
12. The children's Mama and _____ lived in China.
14. Black Chief lost the _____.
16. Grandpa's barnyard was filled with geese, _____, marsh hens, and chicks.
17. 2000 pounds.
20. Paul and Maureen found a _____ bone from the galleon's hull buried in the sand.

The Mouse and the Motorcycle

By Beverly Cleary

SEEK-A-WORD

```
R  L  M  E  H  S  E  C  N  A  L  U  B  M  A
K  I  O  P  O  E  O  I  V  K  L  Q  U  S  M
R  E  L  O  H  T  O  N  K  W  A  E  P  Y  B
H  A  N  D  L  E  B  A  R  R  L  I  W  V  U
R  O  N  U  Q  S  E  W  Y  C  R  Q  O  O  L
O  O  O  A  R  U  I  Q  Y  I  I  S  T  O  T
T  M  O  T  O  O  R  C  N  V  L  H  H  R  E
A  S  T  M  W  M  R  T  E  M  L  E  H  W  R
R  E  E  M  S  O  A  B  E  R  H  E  Y  H  R
E  W  A  S  T  E  B  A  S  K  E  T  Q  V  I
N  R  Y  O  Q  O  R  E  K  N  E  E  I  L  E
I  A  M  W  S  Y  A  V  S  D  D  Y  O  E  R
C  M  A  S  R  E  K  S  I  H  W  W  V  T  K
N  Q  O  V  I  R  Y  R  T  C  W  I  T  O  O
I  S  T  U  N  A  E  P  M  S  E  T  E  H  R
```

WORDS:

Ambulance	Peanuts
Aspirin	Ralph
Handlebar	Ride
Helmet	Room Service
Hotel	Sheet
Incinerator	Terrier
Keith	Toast
Knothole	Towel
Motorcycle	Wastebasket
Mouse	Whiskers

The Mouse and the Motorcycle

By Beverly Cleary

CROSSWORD

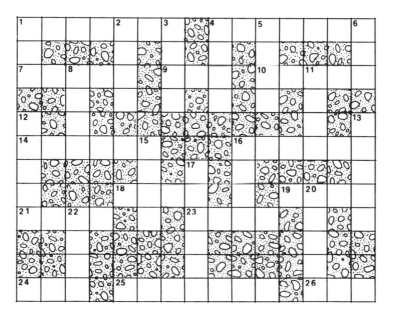

ACROSS

1. Ralph found that he was _____ inside a drinking glass.
4. Keith's parents thought he was sick because he had eaten too many _____.
7. Ralph searched the ground floor for aspirin _____.
9. Keith was Mr. Gridley's _____.
10. Keith let Ralph ride his motorcycle during the _____.
14. Ralph's _____ was a worrier.
16. Ralph loved peanut _____ sandwiches.
18. The mouse _____ in Room 215 was Ralph's home.
19. Keith had hands; Ralph had _____.
21. Ralph parked the ambulance in the elevator behind the man's _____.
23. A sweet, baked food.
24. Keith had a shiny, _____ red motorcycle.
25. Mrs. _____ was certain the hotel had mice.
26. Mice had to be careful not to _____ medicine or poisons.

DOWN

1. Ralph's mother wanted to leave a _____ for Keith's special service.
2. Ralph was carried to the window on a _____ card of a giant redwood tree.
3. The night clerk was not behind the _____ but asleep on a sofa.
4. Keith made Ralph's helmet from a _____-pong ball.
5. Sissy was Ralph's _____.
6. Ralph decided to keep his motorcycle in the lobby under the TV _____.
8. Ralph _____ the wonderful motorcycle in the laundry hamper.
11. The motorcycle was Keith's _____ to Ralph.
12. The motorcycle was too _____ for a boy but just right for a mouse to ride.
13. Ralph hid his _____ helmet behind the curtain.
15. Ralph was the first in his family's history to get _____ service.
16. The terrier's _____ frightened Ralph.
17. Ralph had a tough time getting the pill back to the _____ floor.
20. The boy found the mouse in the wastebasket hiding behind the _____ core.
22. The mouse and the boy wanted to _____ up.

My Brother Sam Is Dead

By James L. Collier

SEEK-A-WORD

```
A  D  W  O  T  R  A  I  D  E  A  D  S  E  S
R  R  E  A  H  S  U  M  S  B  S  I  S  B  B
P  E  I  L  R  N  O  I  T  U  L  O  V  E  R
B  H  R  E  I  A  D  T  L  R  I  N  O  W  O
E  T  H  F  B  R  O  B  O  I  T  U  R  N  W
R  O  O  W  A  N  R  T  Y  N  A  I  B  N  N
A  R  A  T  R  I  E  M  A  N  T  M  R  S  B
M  B  V  E  T  L  T  M  L  C  O  E  H  E  E
T  A  M  I  N  T  E  T  I  A  V  T  T  E  S
P  I  S  A  S  T  B  T  S  A  M  S  A  T  S
R  H  M  D  U  A  O  I  T  R  Y  T  N  L  E
T  I  A  N  P  O  Y  N  E  S  S  E  M  R  B
A  L  I  R  X  N  A  U  L  H  X  A  M  D  E
V  M  I  E  E  S  B  F  O  O  R  L  L  O  A
E  L  E  B  E  R  O  T  E  L  T  T  A  C  Y
```

WORDS:

April
Bayonet
Betsy
British
Brother
Brown Bess
Cattle
Dead
Loyalist
Minuteman

Oxen
Rebel
Revolution
Sam
Shot
Steal
Tavern
Tim
Uniform
War

My Brother Sam Is Dead

By James L. Collier

CROSSWORD

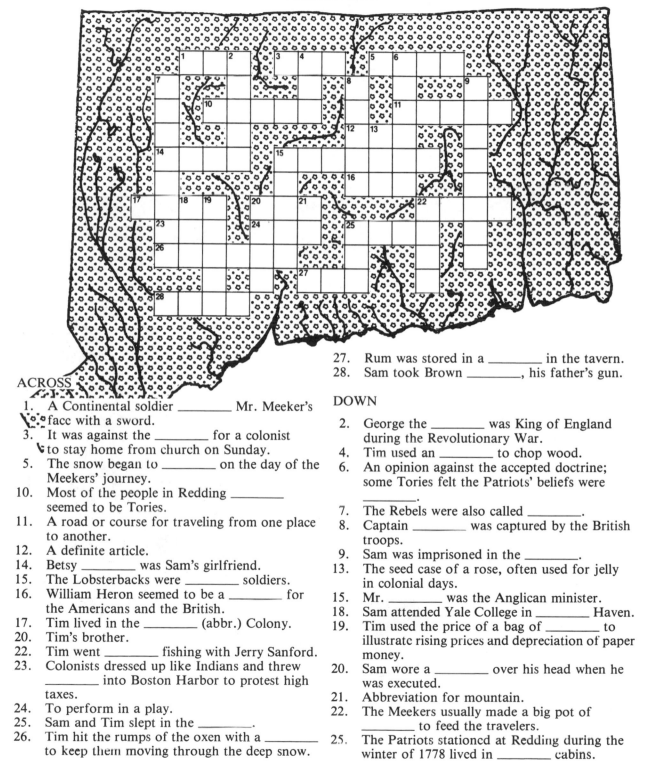

ACROSS

1. A Continental soldier _____ Mr. Meeker's face with a sword.
3. It was against the _____ for a colonist to stay home from church on Sunday.
5. The snow began to _____ on the day of the Meekers' journey.
10. Most of the people in Redding _____ seemed to be Tories.
11. A road or course for traveling from one place to another.
12. A definite article.
14. Betsy _____ was Sam's girlfriend.
15. The Lobsterbacks were _____ soldiers.
16. William Heron seemed to be a _____ for the Americans and the British.
17. Tim lived in the _____ (abbr.) Colony.
20. Tim's brother.
22. Tim went _____ fishing with Jerry Sanford.
23. Colonists dressed up like Indians and threw _____ into Boston Harbor to protest high taxes.
24. To perform in a play.
25. Sam and Tim slept in the _____.
26. Tim hit the rumps of the oxen with a _____ to keep them moving through the deep snow.

27. Rum was stored in a _____ in the tavern.
28. Sam took Brown _____, his father's gun.

DOWN

2. George the _____ was King of England during the Revolutionary War.
4. Tim used an _____ to chop wood.
6. An opinion against the accepted doctrine; some Tories felt the Patriots' beliefs were _____.
7. The Rebels were also called _____.
8. Captain _____ was captured by the British troops.
9. Sam was imprisoned in the _____.
13. The seed case of a rose, often used for jelly in colonial days.
15. Mr. _____ was the Anglican minister.
18. Sam attended Yale College in _____ Haven.
19. Tim used the price of a bag of _____ to illustrate rising prices and depreciation of paper money.
20. Sam wore a _____ over his head when he was executed.
21. Abbreviation for mountain.
22. The Meekers usually made a big pot of _____ to feed the travelers.
25. The Patriots stationed at Redding during the winter of 1778 lived in _____ cabins.

47

Nobody's Family Is Going to Change

By Louise Fitzhugh

SEEK-A-WORD

```
M  I  S  U  C  A  E  D  C  E  W  O  R  D  W
F  L  T  N  H  W  C  F  V  B  L  G  A  M  O
A  Y  H  D  A  L  R  O  A  E  R  A  E  T  R
M  M  G  E  T  Y  L  G  U  E  H  U  M  O  L
Y  M  I  R  N  M  V  H  J  R  T  D  D  E  D
S  P  R  S  I  M  C  I  D  S  T  I  A  Y  F
P  Y  S  T  A  W  L  Y  E  E  A  T  I  K  W
I  S  N  A  L  I  B  E  R  A  T  I  O  N  A
D  E  E  N  P  L  L  I  T  H  T  O  S  L  R
A  I  R  D  M  L  P  Q  C  L  I  N  H  M  E
N  K  D  P  Q  I  A  S  F  A  T  O  A  R  H
C  O  L  A  C  E  M  M  I  W  U  N  R  S  O
E  O  I  T  F  A  M  I  L  Y  D  Y  R  T  U
R  C  H  A  N  G  E  E  D  E  E  L  A  V  S
P  L  C  A  S  S  I  F  I  R  A  L  L  Y  E
```

WORDS:

Attitude
Audition
Change
Children's Rights
Complaint
Cookies
Court
Dancer
Dipsy
Emma

Family
Fat
Female
Lawyer
Liberation
Love
Rally
Understand
Warehouse
Willie

48

Nobody's Family Is Going to Change

By Louise Fitzhugh

CROSSWORD

ACROSS

1. The Children's Army relied upon large _____ of children to confront parents.
6. The "buck wing" is a _____ in tap dancing.
8. Willie thought he'd rather be _____ than never dance.
11. Willie got a job in a Broadway musical _____.
12. Each member of the Army had to bring one _____ of cookies to the meeting.
13. Emma wanted to be _____, not fat.
15. Willie wanted to be a _____ dancer more than anything else.
16. Ketchum, Goldin, and Saunders agreed to _____ Emma in the park.
17. Emma thought her _____ looked like a "brown punching bag."
19. Mr. Sheridan thought his children were _____.
21. Mr. Sheridan wanted Willie to enjoy making a _____ (abbr.) in football.
22. Willie offered to give his father the money from his new _____.
23. Mr. Sheridan wanted his _____ to be a lawyer.
24. Emma imagined her trial outfit to include a big _____ like Bella Abzug's.
25. The Committee investigated a complaint about a mechanical device that toilet-trained _____ wetters.
27. Mr. Sheridan became very _____ every time Dipsey and dancing were mentioned.

28. The Sheridan's maid.
29. Emma found the MERCK _____ on top of the files in her father's office.

DOWN

1. Emma and her three schoolmates were _____ members of the Army.
2. Willie tried dancing _____ the walls like Donald O'Conner in an old movie.
3. Willie wanted to be a star on _____.
4. Abbreviation for "road."
5. To put; place.
6. Nick, the garbage man, showed Willie how to do a _____ step.
7. Harrison Carter warned Emma that all information about the Army was _____ Secret.
9. The Committee investigated the complaint against Mad Dog Madden who broke his son's left _____.
10. Mrs. Sheridan tried to keep Emma on a strict _____.
11. Emma wished that she looked like Gloria _____.
14. MERCK's is a _____ book.
18. Emma often imagined herself in a _____ room trying cases.
20. Mr. Sheridan thought _____ lawyers were fools.
26. Mr. Sheridan was an assistant _____ (abbr.).
27. Ginny was Willie's _____.

Pippi Longstocking
By Astrid Lindgren

SEEK-A-WORD

```
I  K  U  C  I  N  C  I  P  W  O  R  D  N  S
V  C  G  B  T  P  N  A  N  A  R  T  E  O  E
A  F  I  I  P  S  A  Q  I  Y  N  D  G  I  R
E  E  S  R  O  H  O  R  P  I  E  L  A  T  P
W  E  L  T  C  H  R  M  T  W  K  B  C  A  O
T  F  I  H  A  U  E  N  S  Y  I  U  E  C  L
R  F  F  D  R  C  S  L  W  I  C  R  I  A  I
I  O  O  A  T  P  I  P  P  I  H  G  G  V  C
H  C  T  Y  C  A  R  O  L  X  A  L  L  A  E
S  R  F  R  E  C  K  L  E  S  R  A  O  R  M
T  M  O  N  K  E  Y  M  N  O  V  R  O  Y  A
H  S  C  R  E  A  M  P  I  E  E  S  H  T  N
G  P  A  N  C  A  K  E  N  E  N  T  C  F  F
I  S  O  O  S  T  O  C  K  I  N  G  S  H  I
N  S  E  A  C  A  P  T  A  I  N  E  N  I  D
```

WORDS:

Birthday	Pancake
Burglars	Party
Circus	Picnic
Coffee	Pippi
Cream Pie	Policeman
Freckles	School
Horse	Sea Captain
Monkey	Stockings
Nightshirt	Sweden
Nine	Vacation

Pippi Longstocking

By Astrid Lindgren

CROSSWORD

ACROSS

1. Pippi wore brushes on her feet to _____ the kitchen floor.
4. The horse had _____ ribbons braided in his hair.
6. Pippi's father brought her treasures from the Far _____.
8. Pippi's picture showed a woman holding a dead _____.
10. Pippi gave a _____ to the teacher.
12. The _____ shells were in the pancake batter.
14. Pippi threw the coffee pot and cups from the _____ to the ground.
16. One of Pippi's friends.
18. Pippi rescued two boys from a burning skyscraper with a _____.
20. Pippi's age.
22. The robbers were after Pippi's suitcase of _____ pieces.
24. Pippi's father was a _____ captain.

DOWN

2. Pippi wore her _____ in pigtails.
3. Pippi ate all the cream _____ at Mrs. Settergren's coffee party.
5. Malin had enough _____ under her finger-nails to grow a garden!
7. Pippi played _____ with some policemen.
9. Mr. Nilsson went on the picnic and got lost up a pine _____.
11. The woman in Pippi's picture was _____.
13. Pippi enjoyed swinging on the _____ in front of her house.
15. Pippi poured milk in her _____.
17. Pippi never had to _____ her manners.
19. Mrs. Berggren complained that her maid, Rosa, was as dirty as a _____.
21. Mrs. Settergren's maid.
23. It was sometimes hard to tell if Pippi told the truth or _____.

The Pushcart War
By Jean Merrill

SEEK-A-WORD

```
N  P  B  T  G  L  V  R  L  M  Q  C  A  S  S
T  M  A  R  T  R  Q  N  B  L  A  I  P  R  N
S  X  D  A  F  F  O  D  I  L  P  C  E  E  D
T  G  X  C  R  Q  X  M  M  O  G  W  K  L  S
M  I  G  H  T  Y  M  A  M  M  O  T  H  D  S
A  E  S  S  K  P  X  G  B  L  S  I  M  D  W
S  R  O  U  B  I  I  R  F  K  K  G  M  E  T
E  C  R  P  E  B  B  E  L  P  R  E  F  P  R
R  A  F  A  R  K  H  L  T  S  O  R  I  X  A
I  S  K  C  A  T  A  E  P  T  Y  F  N  K  F
T  S  H  B  K  R  T  D  T  W  W  F  F  R  F
T  A  N  N  A  L  A  R  E  N  E  G  O  A  I
A  M  A  F  F  R  U  E  U  B  N  C  R  E  C
L  R  E  W  Q  C  K  A  R  C  G  G  N  A  G
F  A  T  A  E  S  K  C  A  T  K  L  M  G  W
```

WORDS:

Big Mo	Mack	Pea-tack	Tiger
Daffodil	Massacre	Peddlers	Traffic
Flat tires	Maxie	Pushcart	Truce
Frank the Flower	Mighty Mammoth	Tacks	Truck
General Anna	New York	Tax	War

The Pushcart War

By Jean Merrill

CROSSWORD

ACROSS

1. Maxie Hammerman was the _____ King.
4. _____ Portlette was the cleaning lady.
7. The _____ Master Plan was designed by The Three.
9. Wenda Gambling was a movie _____.
11. Frank the Flower had a crocheted truck _____ in jail.
13. Maxie played _____ with The Three and the Police Commissioner.
14. Harry the _____ Dog.
18. _____ was in jail with Frank the Flower.
19. A Mighty _____ truck.
21. Mack was the truck driver who started the _____.
23. Maxie made or repaired _____ the pushcarts.
25. The Pea-Shooter Campaign was only one of the peddlers' _____.
27. The Three planned to _____ Maxie.
28. When Carlos meant "yes," he said, "_____."
31. Pea-tacks were used to "_____" trucks.
32. General Anna sold _____ on her pushcart.
33. The newspapers called the weapons "_____."

DOWN

1. Marvin Seely took a _____ of Mack hitting a pushcart.
2. One of the Commissioner's _____ to the pea-tacks was the one-ton pea order.
3. The _____ pea-pins marked truck hits.
4. _____ Cudd made the Peanut Butter Speech.
5. Hi ya, _____; Hi ya, Bud.
6. The Peace _____ was divided into three divisions.
8. Initials of the peddler who lettered circus carts.
10. "Dead" _____ caused traffic jams.
12. The Flower _____ for Peace ended the Pushcart War.
15. _____ the Florist.
16. Maxie charted the campaign on his city _____.
17. People _____ free food from the pushcarts at the Peace March.
20. Another name for pea-tacks.
21. _____ bought one ton of Posey's Peas.
22. The _____ Tax.
24. The Daffodil Massacre was the _____ event of the War.
26. Hi ya, Daff; hi ya, _____.
29. Initials of the owner of Leaping Lema trucks.
30. Big _____ sold Maxie a bulletproof Italian car (for $14.50!).

Rascal
By Sterling North

SEEK-A-WORD

```
R  A  S  C  C  F  W  S  W  O  W  S  E  R  S
E  R  T  O  O  R  A  O  E  R  O  O  P  W  O
I  C  E  L  I  B  O  M  S  D  L  O  E  O  D
W  N  R  N  O  D  G  C  N  I  E  T  C  S  E
A  D  L  T  S  P  E  S  A  R  L  I  N  S  N
S  L  I  S  K  K  U  N  R  G  F  I  A  H  G
E  U  N  C  K  C  U  A  G  C  E  E  C  O  P
S  S  G  R  O  W  A  N  A  N  O  R  O  A  M
R  U  G  A  I  B  I  B  K  E  O  L  I  P  N
O  E  L  S  R  H  N  O  I  W  D  N  G  F  O
H  C  T  O  S  R  C  M  S  N  R  C  R  A  O
N  E  R  I  O  A  E  H  C  N  I  I  B  C  C
P  O  F  C  A  M  P  I  N  G  E  E  T  R  C
R  L  T  E  L  S  R  S  I  N  T  A  R  E  A
I  S  E  S  R  A  W  C  D  L  A  C  S  A  R
```

WORDS:

Cabin	Poe
Cage	Pets
Camping	Raccoon
Canoe	Rascal
Corn	Skunk
Crow	Sterling
Friend	Sugar
Fishing	Woods
Horses	Wowser
Oldsmobile	Writer

Rascal

By Sterling North

CROSSWORD

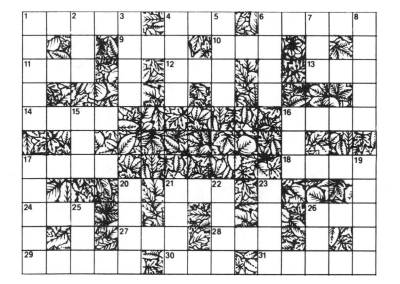

ACROSS

1. Sterling fed his baby raccoon warm milk with a wheat _____.
4. Rascal slept in _____ with Sterling.
6. Rascal tried to wash his first lump of _____ in the bowl of milk.
9. For Christmas Theo gave Sterling a pair of _____ skates.
10. Oscar swiped coffee cake and cookies to _____ on his evening expedition.
11. Rascal liked to eat a turtle _____.
12. Donnybrook _____ faster than Rev. Thurman could drive his Ford.
13. Herschel was Mr. North's _____.
14. Rascal learned how to open the back screen _____ at night.
16. A crow and several skunks were also Sterling's _____.
17. Rascal drank bottles of pop which he held with his hands and _____.
18. Raccoons _____ their food before eating.
21. Rascal loved to drink strawberry _____.
24. Sterling fished with _____ and reel.
26. Sterling and his father lived in a _____-room house.
27. After a fish is caught, a _____ is often used to land it.
28. The water _____ used in making cheese boxes was just right for canoe ribs.
29. Another word for a horse as in "fiery _____."
30. An abbreviation for Saturday.
31. Rascal and Poe fought over a shiny new _____.

DOWN

1. Rascal loved going full _____ down a steep hill in the bike basket.
2. Rascal liked to lie on the jaguar-skin _____.
3. Sterling bought wood and chicken _____ to build Rascal's cage.
4. _____ Bruce introduced Sterling to fly casting.
5. Raccoons' homes are called _____.
6. Sterling liked to eat fried catfish and Mulligan _____.
7. During World War I peach pits were used to make charcoal for _____ masks.
8. Raccoons have _____ on their tails.
15. Rascal weighed less than _____ pound when first found.
16. Rascal fished with his _____.
17. Mr. North owned some _____ in Wisconsin.
19. One of Rascal's favorite delicacies was the _____ at Aunt Lillie's farm.
20. Rascal discovered turtle eggs in the _____.
21. Collecting peach _____ was one of Sterling's war efforts.
22. Jessica was a _____.
23. Mr. North and Sterling made their north woods _____ on a promontory above the Brule River.
25. A female deer.
26. Some of the draft horses at the Irish picnic weighed more than a _____.

Roll of Thunder, Hear My Cry
By Mildred Taylor

SEEK-A-WORD

```
D   R   E   R   O   E   C   E   P   A   C   K   A   R   D

R   A   N   O   G   A   W   X   N   H   U   A   G   S   T

M   E   L   S   X   S   R   D   T   O   N   W   R   T   O

T   H   S   S   I   F   I   R   E   N   X   E   O   X   N

H   R   E   M   T   A   R   X   O   I   P   C   L   E   X

U   A   X   S   O   R   E   T   P   P   S   R   L   H   R

N   F   A   R   E   M   T   P   O   P   O   O   L   E   L

D   I   T   C   H   O   O   R   C   I   O   I   S   O   P

E   A   I   B   C   F   C   A   K   S   M   O   O   S   P

R   O   O   C   H   E   I   P   P   S   C   H   I   S   S

T   O   O   R   R   S   R   U   T   I   C   R   C   R   Y

K   D   I   A   L   O   B   O   A   S   C   I   R   Y   S

A   O   H   A   L   I   R   C   A   S   S   I   E   A   T

R   S   R   T   N   E   A   D   R   I   U   X   E   S   S

L   I   E   G   A   G   T   R   O   M   B   A   R   H   E
```

WORDS:

Book	Mortgage
Bus	Packard
Cassie	Railroad
Cotton	Roll
Cry	School
Ditch	Sharecroppers
Farm	Store
Fire	Taxes
Hear	Thunder
Mississippi	Wagon

Roll of Thunder, Hear My Cry

By Mildred Taylor

CROSSWORD

ACROSS

1. The Logan's most valuable possession.
3. Papa worked on the _____ (abbr.) in Louisiana.
5. Stacey gave his new _____ to T.J.
7. Uncle Hammer's _____ was just like Mr. Granger's.
8. Great _____ Elementary School.
9. The dried calfskin "raincoats" smelled musty when _____.
10. Cassie's grandmother: _____ Ma.
11. Cassie and her brother refused to take their school books because of the _____ stamped inside the cover.
13. Mr. Avery was a _____ on Harlan Granger's land.
14. The Logans lived on a _____.
16. Mr. _____ Tatum called Mr. Barnett a liar.
18. The Logan children were frightened by the _____ riders.
20. Cassie got into trouble in Jim _____'__ Mercantile Store.
22. Little Man tried to keep his new _____ clean on his first day at school.
23. Stacey gave T.J. a black _____ for cheating.
24. Little Man's age.
25. Cassie's grandmother kept a gun under the _____ she shared with Cassie.

DOWN

2. Cassie's people came from _____.
3. The October _____ turned the six-inch layer of dust to red mud.
4. Mr. Jamison's professional field.
5. The Wallaces threatened to send the sheriff after their debtors and put them on the _____ gang.
6. Mrs. Logan was a _____.
7. The first four letters of the city where Hammer lived.
8. Mr. Tatum was covered with tar and _____.
12. T.J. told about the "_____" on the other side of Smellings Creek.
13. Cassie's great-grandpa ran away from _____ three times.
15. The state where Cassie lived. (abbr.)
16. The oldest Logan child.
17. Jack was a _____.
19. Mrs. Logan _____ a cover over the textbook's offensive inside cover.
21. The children dug a ditch across the dirt _____ to stop the bus.

Snow Treasure

By Marie McSwigan

SEEK-A-WORD

```
W   O   N   S   L   E   I   D   R   A   Z   Z   I   L   B
L   F   U   O   O   L   A   A   R   A   D   O   S   G   U
Q   T   R   U   F   G   O   M   W   Z   Y   K   R   S   L
U   Q   R   D   L   N   R   O   S   C   C   K   S   S   L
R   P   P   E   T   E   R   R   H   I   D   E   I   O   I
E   H   H   E   A   S   W   W   R   C   D   K   Z   A   O
R   H   C   A   M   S   B   B   C   R   S   I   Z   A   N
S   S   C   A   M   O   U   F   L   A   G   E   N   A   Z
R   R   H   A   R   Z   U   R   E   V   V   G   A   L   F
E   R   I   H   Z   R   Y   Y   E   A   Z   Z   M   O   U
I   E   L   S   S   A   A   Y   C   A   S   L   E   A   M
D   L   D   W   W   W   A   C   A   L   L   N   N   E   T
L   R   R   Y   R   Y   K   G   N   L   E   N   A   S   W
O   O   E   O   R   O   K   G   O   L   D   T   A   K   R
S   S   N   O   W   M   A   N   O   S   S   K   S   E   E
```

WORDS:

Blizzard
Bricks
Bullion
Camouflage
Cave
Children
Gold
Helga
Hide
Nazis

Norway
Peter
Riswyk
School
Skis
Sleds
Snake
Snowman
Soldiers
Treasure

Snow Treasure

By Marie McSwigan

CROSSWORD

ACROSS

2. _____ was a tomboy.
4. The cold waters of the fiords were filled with floating _____ chunks.
6. Lieutenant "Sit-_____" had trouble skiing.
8. Bullion is _____ before it is made into money.
9. Peter was president of the Defense _____.
11. The children built _____ men over the gold.
14. Where the gold was hidden.
15. An "epidemic" kept the children home from _____.
17. Town where *Snow Treasure* takes place.
20. Each gold brick weighed 18½ _____.
21. Unit of Norwegian money.
22. Thirteen _____ of bullion equalled nine million dollars.
25. Each child carried gold on his/her _____.
28. _____ almost ruined their plans for moving the gold.
29. Number of teams of children.
30. Color of the Nazi uniforms.
31. Uncle Victor made his living from the _____.
32. The _____ was a twisted arm of the Riswyk Fiord.

DOWN

1. The Nazis "goose-stepped" with stiff _____.
2. The children spent nights with Fru and Herr _____.
3. It is winter much of the year in the _____ Circle.
5. Per Garson's bones predicted a _____ in the weather.
7. Capital of Norway.
10. Each gold _____ was wrapped in a sack.
12. Each "sick" child was covered with many of these.
13. Uncle Victor took Jan and Peter to the _____ (abbr.).
16. Peter's father's name.
17. The gold was hidden near Thor's _____.
18. The Cleng Peerson was Victor's _____.
19. Louvisa almost started to _____ when the German Commandant threatened her.
20. _____ hit the German Commandant on the ear with a snowball.
22. Peter's age.
23. The gold was taken to the United _____ for safekeeping.
24. Fir trees were used as camouflage to _____ the ship.
26. _____ of the children spoke to the German soldiers.
27. *Snow Treasure* is based on a _____ story.

59

Sounder
By William Armstrong

SEEK-A-WORD

```
X  E  I  P  P  I  T  L  X  S  D  O  G  G  E
U  U  N  N  E  R  N  A  M  E  A  A  H  I  T
Q  Q  O  Y  B  O  O  D  L  J  S  H  F  W  A
N  U  G  J  F  F  O  P  A  G  A  U  H  S  E
S  I  A  O  A  R  P  M  S  S  T  U  E  N
H  W  W  R  A  I  O  L  R  R  E  H  T  A  F
E  C  H  A  R  D  L  T  E  A  C  H  E  R  U
R  T  N  C  L  Y  E  R  D  O  N  M  N  C  S
I  N  U  H  U  N  O  D  N  G  H  A  N  H  I
F  N  S  S  O  O  U  B  U  B  Y  C  U  A  B
F  U  O  G  A  W  L  T  O  C  S  N  Y  Q  N
M  M  E  G  A  S  U  A  S  O  T  K  G  O  I
H  E  H  A  G  U  S  S  A  O  K  T  I  N  B
Y  N  A  A  I  T  E  M  N  N  S  C  A  B  A
D  Y  N  A  M  I  T  E  E  O  K  U  I  N  C
```

WORDS:

Book	Jail
Boy	Mush
Cabin	Quarry
Coon	Sausage
Crippled	Search
Dog	Sheriff
Dynamite	Sounder
Father	Teacher
Ham	Wagon
Hunt	Walnuts

Sounder

By William Armstrong

CROSSWORD

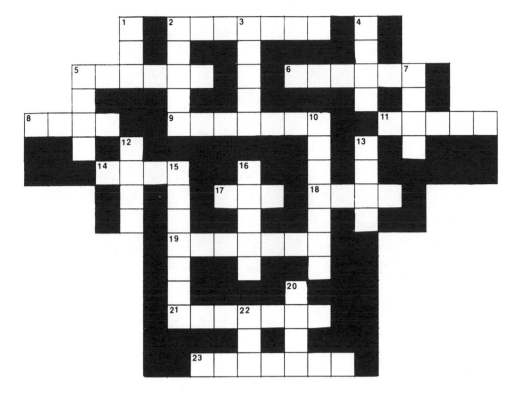

ACROSS

2. The _____ taught the boy to read.
5. The boy spent the _____ months working in the fields.
6. One of the most important Southern field crops.
8. The father was sentenced to work on a chain _____.
9. The name of the dog.
11. The boy's mattress was made of _____.
14. The boy loved to _____ at night with his father and the dog.
17. The book was written from the point of view of the _____.
18. One day the boy found a _____ in a trash can.
19. The mother worked in the _____ of the big house down the road.
21. The boy had patches of this material on his overall knees.
23. The father always carried a special _____ when he hunted at night.

DOWN

1. The sheriff took the father to jail because he stole a _____.
2. The woods around the house were filled with jack oak, cottonwood, and pine _____.
3. Type of house where the boy lived.
4. Deep marks in the dirt road made by wagon wheels.
5. When she was worried, the mother's favorite _____ was "That Lonesome Road."
7. The mother picked out and sold _____ for extra money.
10. Sounder was a _____ hound.
12. When hunting was bad, the mother made corn meal _____ for the children to eat.
13. The boy and his father hunted this animal.
15. The father's overalls were patched with striped _____.
16. The crippled man and the old dog often sat together on the _____ steps.
20. The boy took this present to his father.
22. The sheriff threatened the boy and his family with a _____.

Take Wing
By Jean Little

SEEK-A-WORD

```
S  H  C  R  E  H  B  R  E  T  A  R  D  E  D
Y  P  E  T  S  R  E  T  S  M  A  H  T  H  A
A  L  N  L  U  R  B  D  S  T  O  O  R  T  W
L  U  O  O  P  G  N  S  S  E  Y  R  A  H  H
A  C  C  I  D  E  N  T  G  A  E  O  O  T  L
T  S  C  H  I  H  L  A  L  K  C  O  E  T  S
L  N  U  R  R  S  I  P  A  E  A  P  T  H  S
E  D  F  F  C  U  E  E  S  N  S  E  P  S  A
R  D  E  H  D  R  R  U  S  L  D  S  E  L  M
U  R  O  I  R  B  O  A  E  A  Q  U  A  L  T
A  O  C  M  D  H  R  E  S  E  M  A  J  T  S
L  C  L  N  E  T  R  B  S  R  S  H  R  I  I
A  L  I  H  N  O  T  T  U  B  T  C  A  L  R
H  W  I  N  D  O  S  A  T  M  E  B  R  E  H
T  O  O  T  L  T  R  A  L  T  X  A  T  T  C
```

WORDS:

Accident	Housecoat
Aunt	James
Button	Laurel
Christmas	Play
Elspeth	Retarded
Friends	School
Glasses	Toothbrush
Hamster	Windbreaker
Help	
Herb	

Take Wing

By Jean Little

CROSSWORD

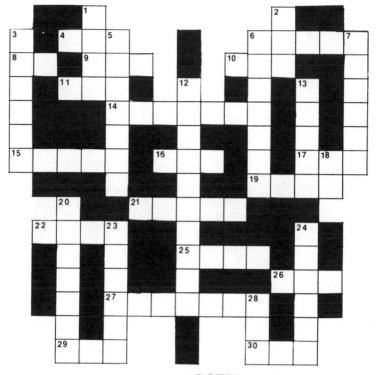

ACROSS

4. James' good coat had _____ buttons.
6. _____ was Laurel's retarded brother.
8. Initials of Laurel's cousin.
9. Laurel liked to dream she could _____.
10. James and his dad shared his dad's _____.
11. Parent Teacher Association (abbr.).
14. Laurel told James _____ about the Teeny Tiny Woman.
15. The color of Aunt Jessica's mouse.
16. James still _____ his bed.
17. The Canadian winter _____ is crisp and cold.
19. Laurel called her _____ to come and help out.
21. Barbara was Laurel's _____ study in the class play.
22. The hamster's name.
25. _____ helped James make snowballs.
26. The province where Laurel lived (abbr.).
27. _____ went to a private school.
29. The children were _____ on Christmas Eve until Mrs. Ross came home.
30. Aunt Jessica had a mouse for a _____ when she was a little girl.

DOWN

1. Title of the class play: "The Secret _____."
2. James' _____ took him to the Mental Health Clinic.
3. Puff's color.
5. Laurel sometimes called James "Owl" because of his thick _____.
6. Susan and _____ were sisters.
7. Alice was Barbara's _____.
12. "A _____ is a fragile thing."
13. Elspeth's aunt.
18. The Teeny Tiny Woman always shouted, "Take _____!"
20. Laurel practiced with the _____ of her housecoat.
23. Laurel wanted to be Barbara's _____.
24. Lindsay's nickname.
28. Mrs. Ross fell and broke her _____.

A Wrinkle in Time

By Madeleine L'Engle

SEEK-A-WORD

```
M  E  G  M  A  J  R  N  M  P  S  X  R  V  W
R  R  G  R  K  P  A  C  O  S  T  B  U  R  R
S  C  S  S  C  L  B  K  A  E  R  C  E  W  H
W  L  H  W  W  R  I  N  K  L  E  G  T  R  Y
H  A  S  H  H  E  F  L  Z  R  N  W  A  W  T
O  S  M  I  H  A  I  E  I  A  X  V  O  S  H
Z  S  I  C  I  U  T  W  D  H  Y  Z  I  C  M
V  I  T  H  D  N  B  S  C  C  A  L  V  I  N
E  F  R  C  E  T  U  R  I  E  L  Y  T  E  X
I  I  W  H  A  B  R  I  E  T  I  H  H  N  F
T  E  Z  O  T  E  D  N  G  E  K  R  E  T  A
R  D  Q  U  E  A  A  L  O  V  E  V  D  I  T
L  G  L  A  S  S  E  S  E  S  S  G  L  S  H
A  B  O  U  T  T  C  A  R  E  S  S  E  T  E
C  A  M  A  Z  O  T  Z  T  O  Y  D  A  B  R
```

WORDS:

Alike
Aunt Beast
Calvin
Camazotz
Charles
Classified
Danger
Father
Glasses
It

Love
Meg
Mrs. Whatsit
Mrs. Which
Mrs. Who
Rhythm
Scientist
Tesseract
Uriel
Wrinkle

A Wrinkle in Time

By Madeleine L'Engle

CROSSWORD

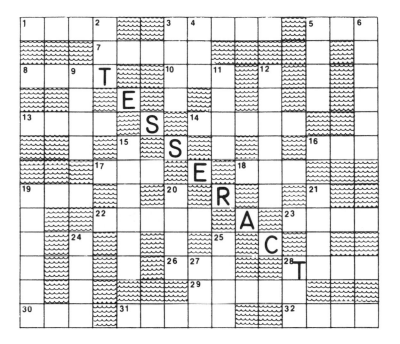

ACROSS

1. The improbable nickname Mrs. Whatsit gave Mrs. Murry.
3. Everyone, except his family, thought Charles Wallace was a _____.
5. The first three letters of the dark planet's name.
7. Planet of the beautiful creatures.
8. It promised everyone peace and _____.
10. Opposite of subtract.
13. The color of everything on Ixchel.
14. The _____ dimension is a tesseract.
16. The creatures on Ixchel could not _____, but sensed with their tentacles.
17. Fortinbras was the Murry's _____.
18. The person who rescued Charles Wallace.
19. Sandy's age.
22. Meg wrapped herself in an old patch-work _____ and listened to the storm.
23. Charles Wallace moved the _____s of the wall for Meg and Calvin to walk through.
26. Mrs. _____.
28. Sandy had a _____ brother.
29. Everyone on the dark planet was programmed to be _____.
30. The color of Calvin's hair.

31. A creature of Ixchel.
32. Meg called the Thing who cared for her "_____ Beast."

DOWN

2. A conjunction.
3. The "_____" that Meg ate tasted like turkey.
4. Mrs. Which was very _____.
5. The Happy Medium lived in a _____.
6. The hall of CENTRAL was made of green _____.
9. Mrs. Whatsit was once a _____.
11. The brain was on top of a round _____.
12. Charles Wallace was searching for his _____.
15. Mr. Murry was trapped in a transparent _____.
19. To "Wrinkle" time.
20. The wind _____ hard during the storm.
21. Mrs. Murry cooked _____ for her family and Calvin.
24. The way Meg felt when she traveled through the Thing.
25. Meg left the fifth dimension with a _____.
27. Form of the verb "have."
28. One of the beverages the Happy Medium offered.

ANSWERS

The Black Stallion
By Walter Farley

SEEK-A-WORD

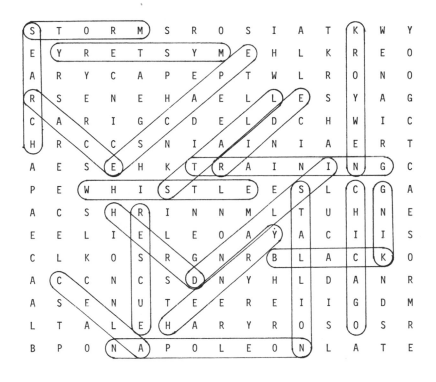

CROSSWORD

Blubber

By Judy Blume

SEEK-A-WORD

CROSSWORD

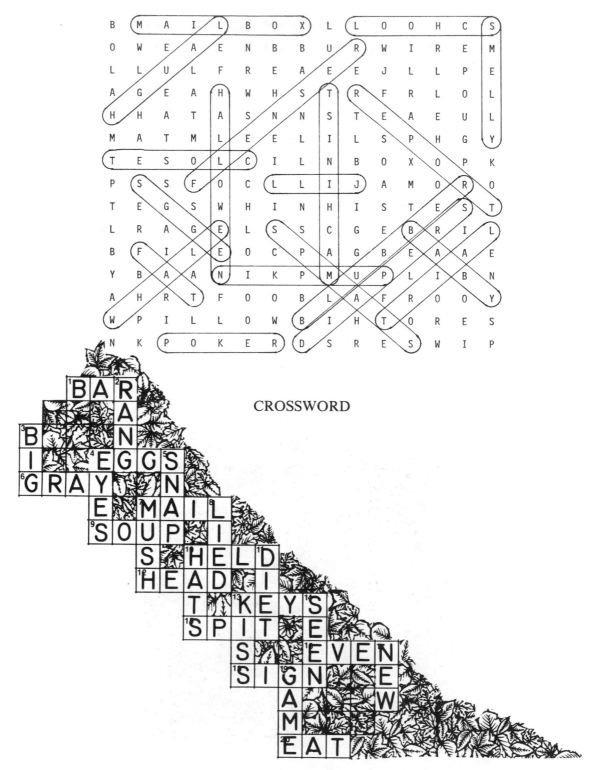

The Bridge to Terabithia

By Katherine Paterson

SEEK-A-WORD

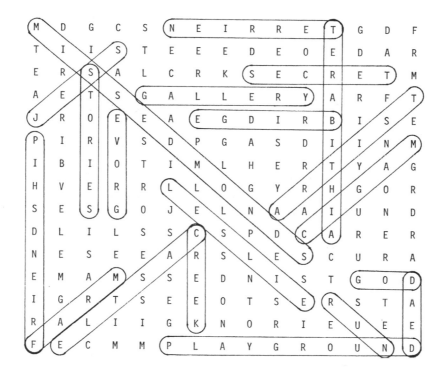

CROSSWORD

Charlotte's Web

By E. B. White

SEEK-A-WORD

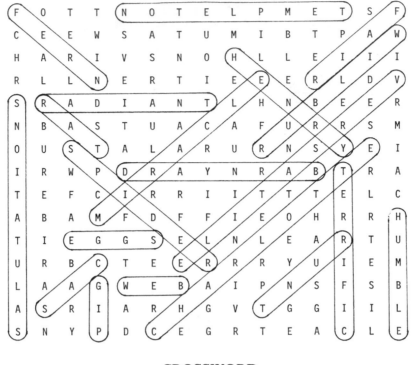

CROSSWORD

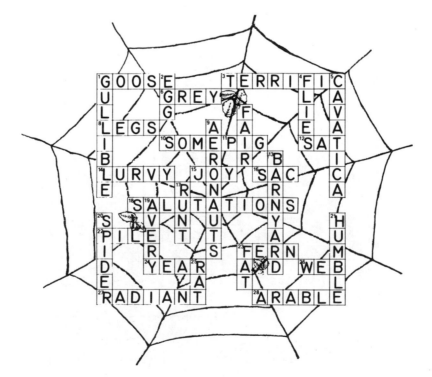

Dorp Dead
By Julia Cunningham

SEEK-A-WORD

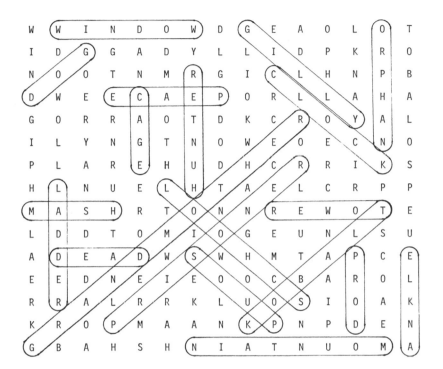

CROSSWORD

The Egypt Game

By Zilpha Snyder

SEEK-A-WORD

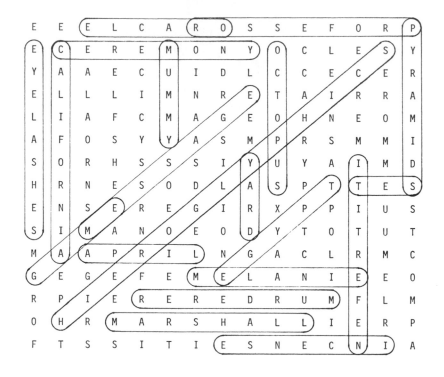

CROSSWORD

74

Freaky Friday
By Mary Rodgers

SEEK-A-WORD

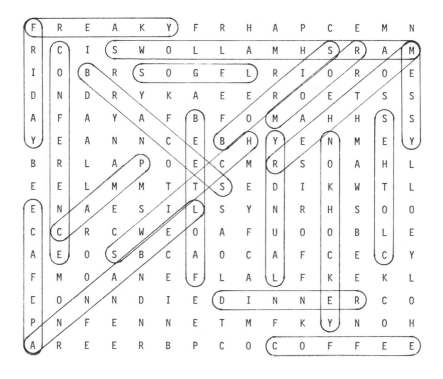

CROSSWORD

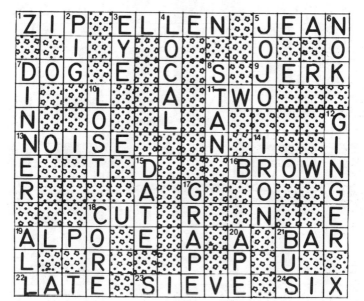

From the Mixed-Up Files of
Mrs. Basil E. Frankweiler

By E. L. Konigsburg

SEEK-A-WORD

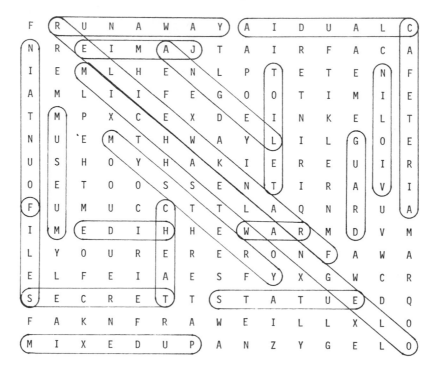

CROSSWORD

Henry Reed's Journey

By Keith Robertson

SEEK-A-WORD

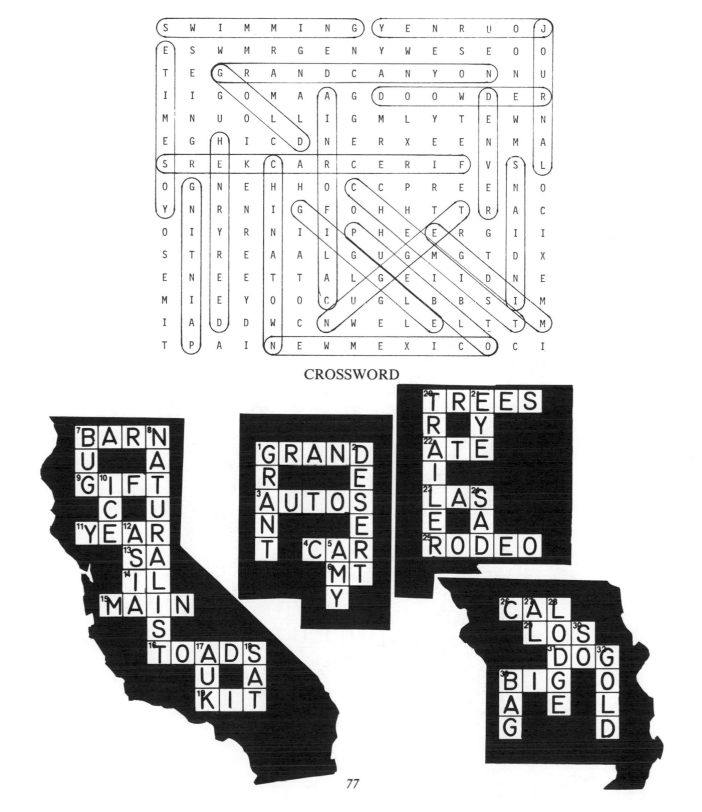

CROSSWORD

Island of the Blue Dolphins
By Scott O'Dell

SEEK-A-WORD

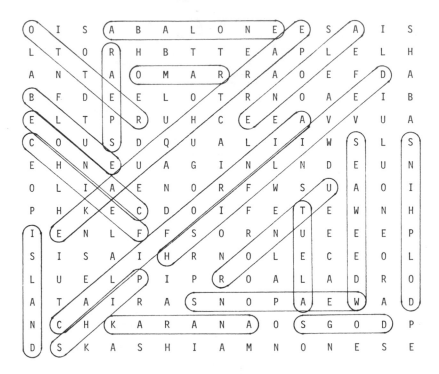

CROSSWORD

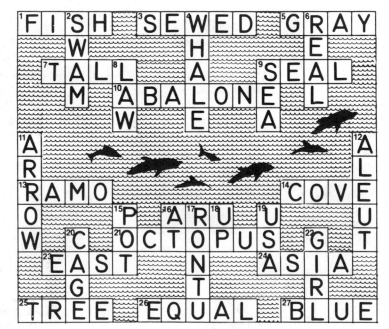

Julie of the Wolves

By Jean George

SEEK-A-WORD

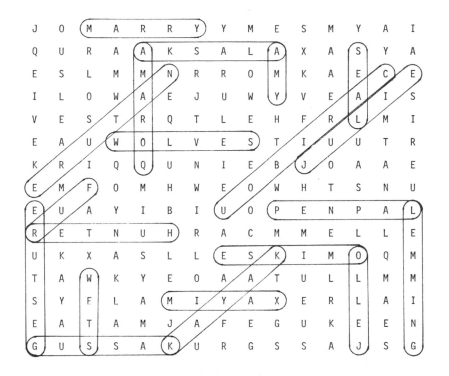

```
J O M A R R Y Y M E S M Y A I
Q U R A A K S A L A X A S Y A
E S L M M N R R O M K A E C E
I L O W A E J U W Y V E A I S
V E S T R Q T L E H F R L M I
E A U W O L V E S T I U U T R
K R I Q U N I E B J O A A E E
E M F O M H W E O W H T S N U
E U A Y I B I U O P E N P A L
R E T N U H R A C M M E L L E
U K X A S L L E S K I M O Q M
T A W K Y E O A A T U L L M M
S Y F L A M I Y A X E R L A I
E A T A M J A F E G U K E E N
G U S S A K U R G S S A J S G
```

CROSSWORD

```
Z I T   K A P U G E N   S E A
A   E   A   L   I   S L   M Y
T   N   Y   O   G   L E   Y
        K       H   E
    T E A M     S H E D
I   E   K   T           C
N A I L S       S E D G E
D               E       L
I C E           O W L   L
A               H       A
N U S A N   C O L O R S  
S   N       H           R
    E   D E E R   N A I T
D E E D E L   A   R   N E
N A P E S K I M O S   P O T
```

Little House in the Big Woods

By Laura Ingalls Wilder

SEEK-A-WORD

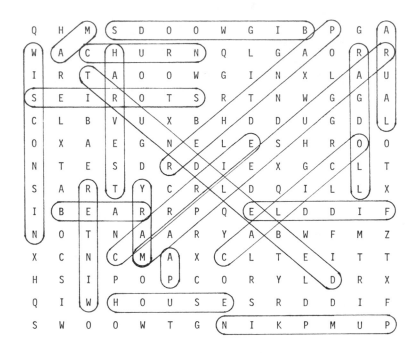

CROSSWORD

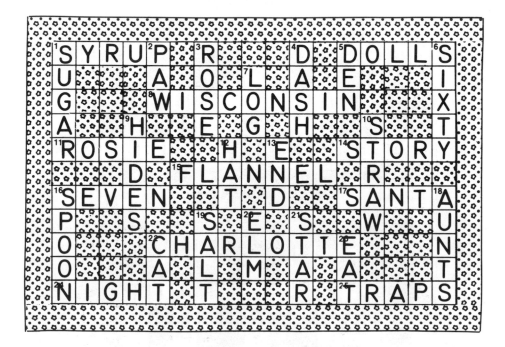

Mary Poppins
By P. L. Travers

SEEK-A-WORD

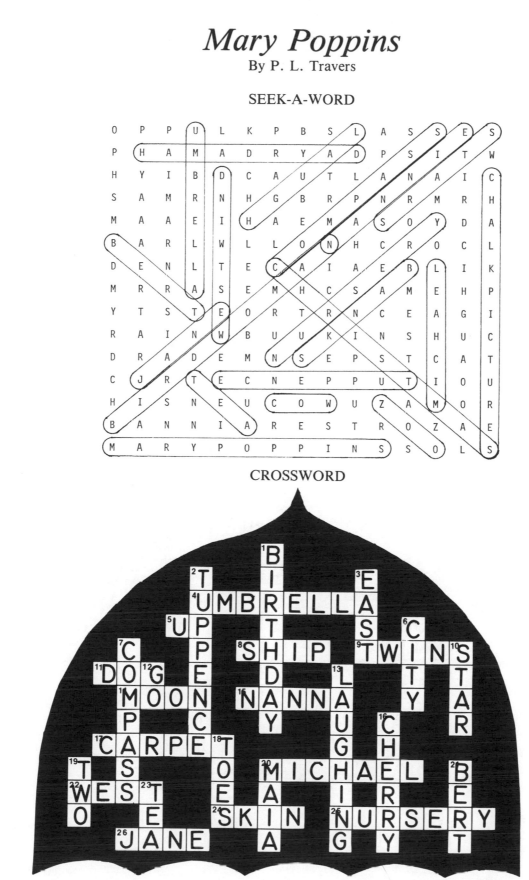

CROSSWORD

Misty of Chincoteague

By Marguerite Henry

SEEK-A-WORD

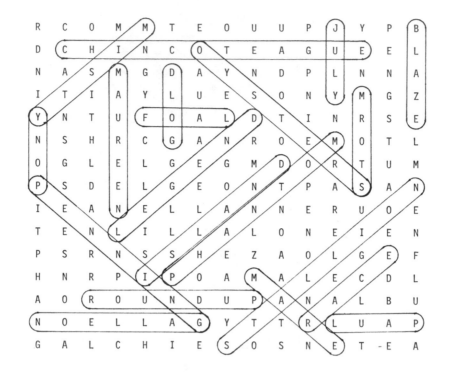

```
R C O M M T E O U U P   J Y P   B
  C H I N C O T E A G U E   E     L
D A S M G D A Y N D P L   N   N   A
I T I A Y L U E S O N Y   M   G   Z
Y N T U F O A L D T I N   R   S   E
N S H R C G A N R O E   M R   T   L
O G L E L G E G M D O R   T   U   M
P S D E L G E O N T P A   S   A   N
I E A N E L L A N N E R U O   E   E
T E N L I L L A L O N E I E N   F
P S R N S S H E Z A O L G E   L
H N R P I P O A M A L E C D   L
A O R O U N D U P A N A L B U
N O E L L A G Y T T R L U A P
G A L C H I E S O S N E T - E A
```

CROSSWORD

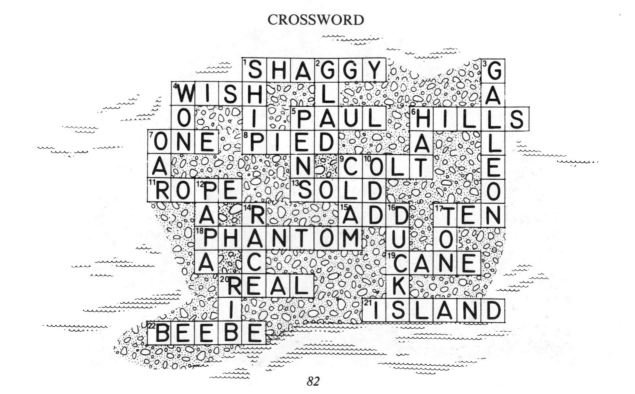

The Mouse and the Motorcycle
By Beverly Cleary

SEEK-A-WORD

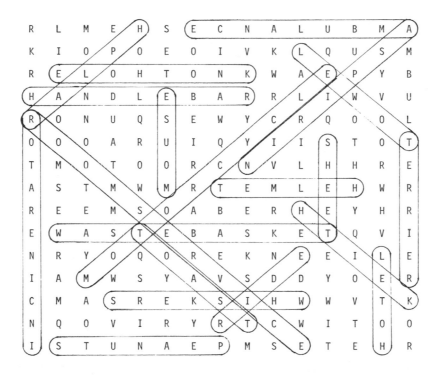

CROSSWORD

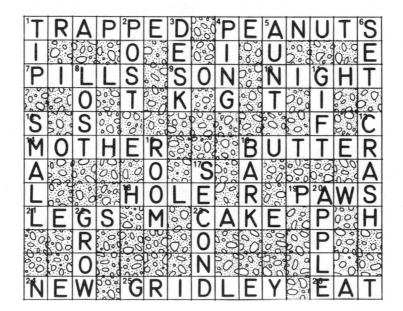

My Brother Sam Is Dead

By James L. Collier

SEEK-A-WORD

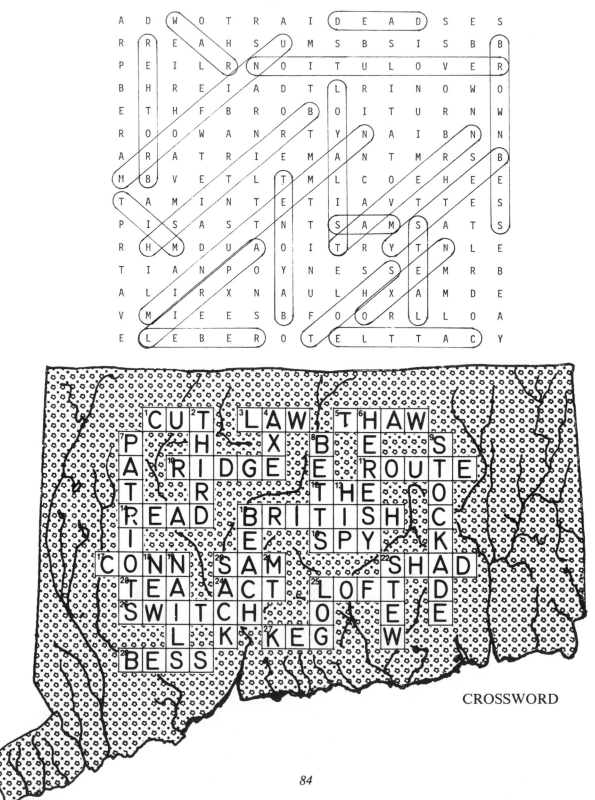

CROSSWORD

84

Nobody's Family Is Going to Change

By Louise Fitzhugh

SEEK-A-WORD

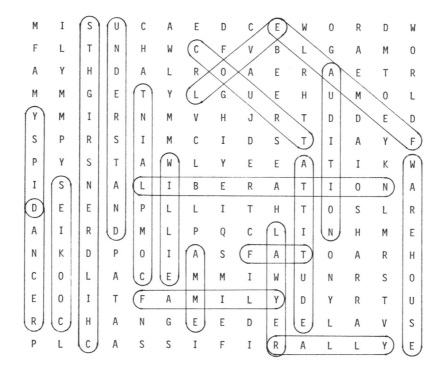

CROSSWORD

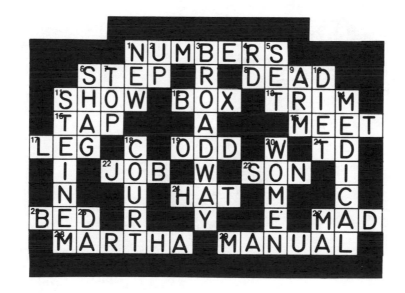

Pippi Longstocking
By Astrid Lindgren

SEEK-A-WORD

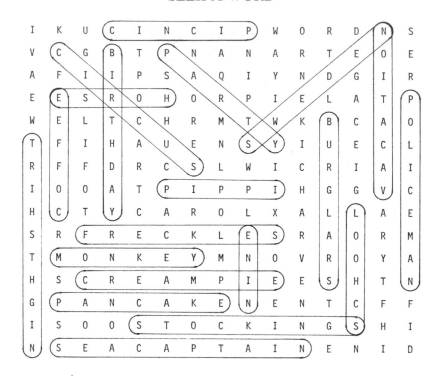

CROSSWORD

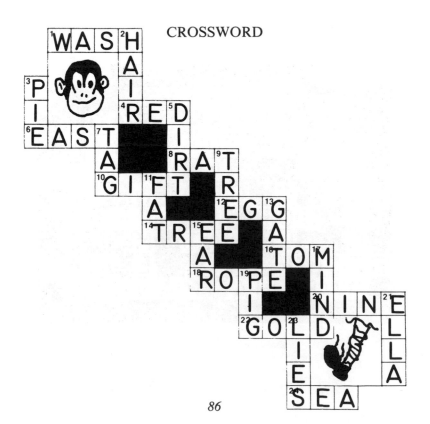

The Pushcart War

By Jean Merrill

SEEK-A-WORD

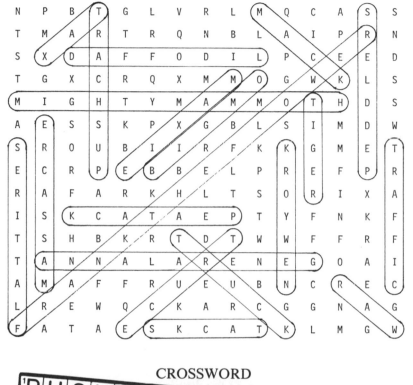

CROSSWORD

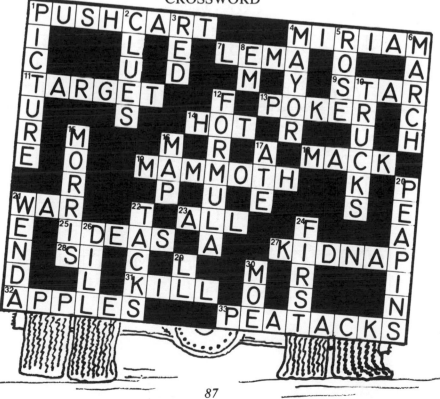

Rascal

By Sterling North

SEEK-A-WORD

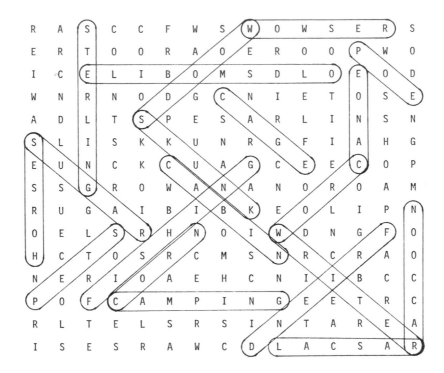

CROSSWORD

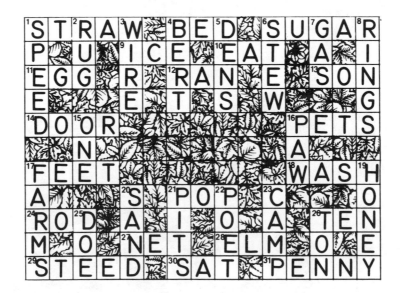

Roll of Thunder, Hear My Cry

By Mildred Taylor

SEEK-A-WORD

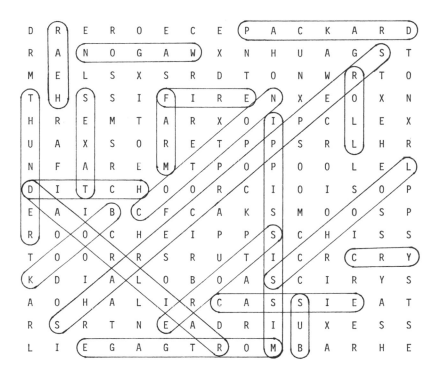

CROSSWORD

Snow Treasure

By Marie McSwigan

SEEK-A-WORD

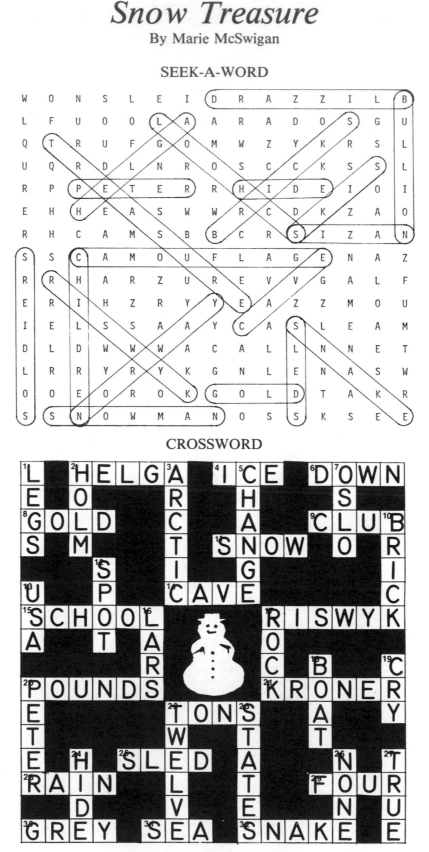

CROSSWORD

90

Sounder

By William Armstrong

SEEK-A-WORD

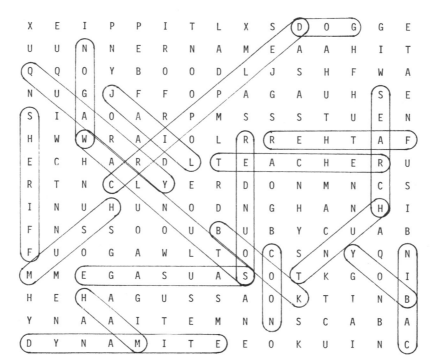

CROSSWORD

Take Wing

By Jean Little

SEEK-A-WORD

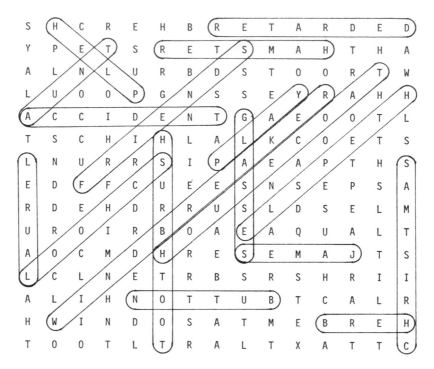

CROSSWORD

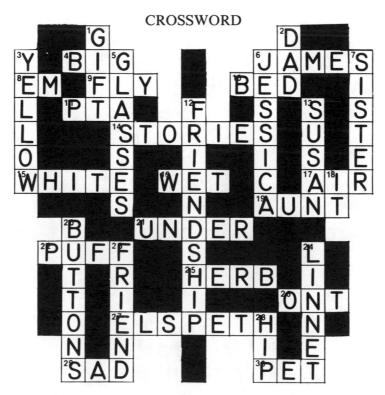

A Wrinkle in Time

By Madeleine L'Engle

SEEK-A-WORD

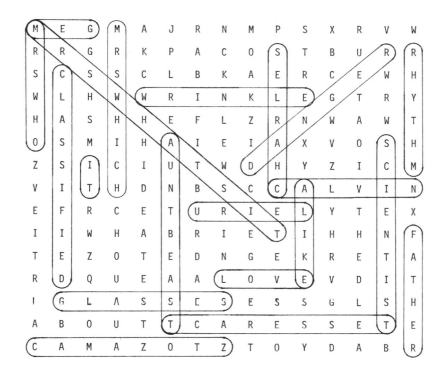

CROSSWORD

INDEXES

Index of Recommended Grade Levels
by Puzzle Title

Index of Puzzles by Recommended Grade Level

BIBLIOGRAPHY

Armstrong, William. *Sounder*. Harper, 1969. Pap. ed. Harper, 1972.

Blume, Judy. *Blubber*. Bradbury, 1974. Pap. ed. Dell, 1976, 1978.

Cleary, Beverly. *The Mouse and the Motorcycle*. Morrow, 1965. Pap. ed. Dell, 1980.

Collier, James L., and Christopher Collier. *My Brother Sam Is Dead*. Four Winds, 1974. Pap. ed. Scholastic, 1977.

Cunningham, Julia. *Dorp Dead*. Pantheon, 1965. Pap. ed. Avon, 1974, 1980.

Farley, Walter. *The Black Stallion*. Random House, 1941. Pap. ed. Random, 1977.

Fitzhugh, Louise. *Nobody's Family Is Going to Change*. Farrar, Straus, 1974. Pap. ed. Dell, 1975.

George, Jean. *Julie of the Wolves*. Harper, 1972. Pap. ed. Harper, n.d.

Henry, Marguerite. *Misty of Chincoteague*. Rand McNally, 1947. Pap. ed. Rand, n.d.

Konigsburg, E. L. *From the Mixed-Up Files of Mrs. Basil E. Frankweiler*. Atheneum, 1967. Pap. ed. Atheneum, n.d.; Dell, 1977.

L'Engle, Madeleine. *A Wrinkle in Time*. Farrar, Straus, 1962. Pap. ed. Dell, 1973.

Lindgren, Astrid. *Pippi Longstocking*. Viking, 1950. Pap. ed. Penguin, 1977.

Little, Jean. *Take Wing*. Little, 1968.

McSwigan, Marie. *Snow Treasure*. Dutton, 1942. Pap. ed. Scholastic, n.d.

Merrill, Jean. *The Pushcart War*. Young Scott, 1964. Pap. ed. Dell, 1978.

North, Sterling. *Rascal*. Dutton, 1963. Pap. ed. Avon, 1969.

O'Dell, Scott. *Island of the Blue Dolphins*. Houghton, 1960. Pap. ed. Dell, 1978.

Paterson, Katherine. *The Bridge to Terabithia*. Crowell, 1977. pap. ed. Avon, 1979.

Robertson, Keith. *Henry Reed's Journey*. Viking, 1963. Pap. ed. Grosset, 1967; Dell, 1974.

Rodgers, Mary. *Freaky Friday*. Harper, 1972. Pap. ed. Harper, 1973, 1977.

Snyder, Zilpha. *The Egypt Game*. Atheneum, 1967. Pap. ed. Atheneum, 1972.

Taylor, Mildred. *Roll of Thunder, Hear My Cry*. Dial, 1976. Pap. ed. Bantam, 1978.

Travers, P. L. *Mary Poppins*. Harcourt, 1962. Pap. ed. Harcourt, 1972.

White, E. B. *Charlotte's Web*. Harper, 1952. Pap. ed. Harper, 1952.

Wilder, Laura Ingalls. *Little House in the Big Woods*. Harper, 1953. Pap. ed. Harper, n.d.